Joshua James Likes
TRUCKS

By
Catherine
Petrie

Illustrated by
Joel Snyder

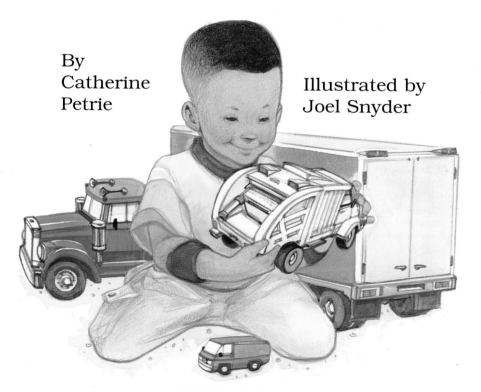

SCHOLASTIC INC.

New York   Toronto   London   Auckland   Sydney
Mexico City   New Delhi   Hong Kong   Buenos Aires

For Luke
—C.P.

READING CONSULTANTS
Linda Cornwell
Coordinator of School Quality and Professional Improvement
(Indiana State Teachers Association)

Katharine A. Kane
Education Consultant
(Retired, San Diego County Office of Education and San Diego State University)

9   10   11   12   62   11

Joshua James likes trucks.

Big trucks,

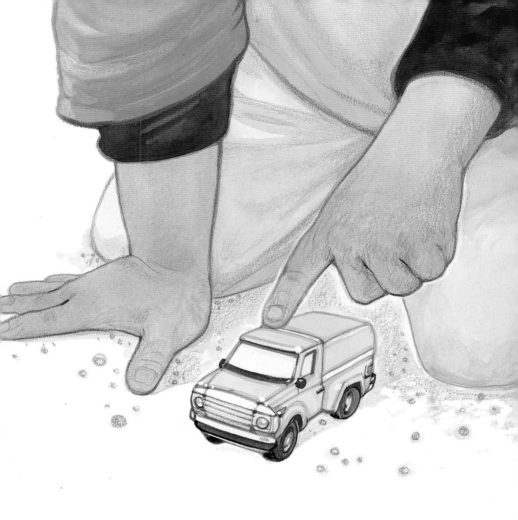

little trucks,

long trucks,

short trucks.

Joshua James just likes trucks!

9

Red trucks,

green trucks,

yellow trucks,

blue trucks.

Joshua James just likes trucks.

Trucks that go up.

Trucks that go down.

Trucks that go round and round.

Joshua James just likes trucks.

Word List (19 words)

and	Joshua	short
big	just	that
blue	likes	trucks
down	little	up
go	long	yellow
green	red	
James	round	

About the Author

Catherine Petrie is a reading specialist with a Master of Science degree in Reading. She taught reading in the public schools and her experience made her aware of the lack of material currently available for the emergent reader. Her creative use of a limited vocabulary based on high-frequency sight words, combined with the frequent repetition and rhyming word families, provide the emergent reader with a positive independent reading experience.

About the Illustrator

A graduate of The Rhode Island School of Design, Joel Snyder lives and works in his home in upstate New York. Having recently restored his 150-year-old Gothic Revival home, Joel does what he was born to do—fish, illustrate, and give lots of TLC to his young son, Adam.

Praise for the
Murder-by-Month Series

"Move over, Stephanie Plum. There's a new bad girl in town, and her name is Mira James. The funny, earthy heroine of *June Bug* is sure to stumble her way into the hearts of readers everywhere. With a keen eye to the bawdy side of life, Jess Lourey delivers a story that's loonier than our state bird; with a deft hand, she both celebrates and skewers the myths about straight-laced life in small-town Minnesota. Don't miss this one—it's a hoot!"

—Wlliam Kent Krueger,
Anthony Award–winning author of *Copper River*

"Mira is young, sexy, enthusiastic, and—like all amateur sleuths—forever doomed to find the bodies of the recently departed . . . Jess Lourey is a talented, witty, and clever writer."

—Monica Ferris, best-selling author of the Needlecraft Mysteries

"With just the right amount of insouciance, tongue-in-cheek sexiness, and plain common sense, Jess Lourey offers up a funny, well-written, engaging story."

—Carl Brookins, author of *The Case of the Greedy Lawyers*

"All the ingredients for a successful small-town cozy series are here."

—*Publishers Weekly*

"What a romp this is! . . . I found myself laughing out loud."

—*Crimespree Magazine*

"Meet this witty heroine in Lourey's engaging new series."

—*Mystery Scene Magazine*

"Lourey's debut has a likable heroine and a surfeit of sass."

—*Kirkus Reviews*

"You gotta love a heroine who is not only addicted to Nut Goodies but also tells a newbie how to eat one."

—*Saint Paul Pioneer Press*

"Nut Goodies serve as an ideal metaphor for Lourey's writing . . . sweet, nutty, evocative of the American Heartland, and utterly addicting."

—*The Strand*

"Mira is the strength of the book. She has a unique voice, full of irreverent humor . . . I couldn't help rooting for [her]."

—*All About Romance*

"*May Day* starts the action rolling with a clever mystery and some snappy writing . . . These pages are filled with fresh dialogue . . . an offbeat mystery."

—*In the Library*

"Jess Lourey writes about a small-town assistant librarian, but this is no genteel traditional mystery . . . She flees a dead-end job and a dead-end boyfriend in Minneapolis and lands up in Battle Lake, a little town with plenty of dirty secrets. The first-person narrative in *May Day* is fresh, the characters quirky. Minnesota has many fine crime writers, and Jess Lourey has just entered their ranks!"

—Ellen Hart, author of the Jane Lawless mystery series

"Lourey knows her turf."

—Peter Handel, *Pages*

"Jess Lourey writes a light-hearted murder mystery, and she writes it well."

—Who-dunnit.com

"This trade paperback packed a lot of punch . . . I loved it from the get-go!"

—*Tulsa World*

june
bug

ALSO BY JESS LOUREY

May Day

FORTHCOMING BY JESS LOUREY

Knee High by the 4th of July

june
bug

MURDER by
Month
Mystery

Jess Lourey

To
Mary

MIDNIGHT INK
WOODBURY, MINNESOTA

FIRST EDITION
First Printing, 2007

Book design by Donna Burch
Cover design by Lisa Novak
Cover illustration © 2006 by Yuki Hatori / CWC International, Inc.

Midnight Ink, an imprint of Llewellyn Publications

Library of Congress Cataloging-in-Publication Data
The Cataloging-in-Publication Data for *June Bug: A Murder-by-Month Mystery* is on file at the Library of Congress.
ISBN-13: 978-0-7387-0912-3
ISBN-10: 0-7387-0912-3

Midnight Ink
Llewellyn Publications
2143 Wooddale Drive, Dept. 0-7387-0912-3
Woodbury, MN 55125-2989, U.S.A.
www.midnightinkbooks.com

Printed in the United States of America

For Zoë and Xander,
who better not read it until they're 18;
thank you both for being perfect, every day

ONE

In my dream, I walked days and nights through the woods to reach the clear stream. A tower built to look like a silo loomed at the water's edge, and I knew I was home. The creek gurgled, the moon shone, and the frog sounds of night sang to me. I laid down to rest and was swept with serenity. There was warm breath on the back of my neck and a comforting hand on my shoulder. I felt protected, covered in the safety of night and cozy warmth. But when the hand crept purposefully lower and I smelled digesting Schlitz on the tepid breath, I knew I wasn't in paradise anymore. My body lurched awake, and I was standing before I even remembered I had been lying down. The vertigo caught up with me, and I clutched at a bedpost as I blinked rapidly.

"What!" I yelled.

"Sunny?" slurred the voice in my bed.

I shook my head and some REM-spun cobwebs fell out. I wasn't in my apartment in Minneapolis, where I had lived for nearly ten years—a little loft on the West Bank where I'd shared a bathroom with a sexy, blue-eyed horn player in his sixties and a compulsively clean law student. I had moved out of there in March, leaving my cheating boyfriend and my career as a waitress and grad student in the University of Minnesota English program, and had been house-sitting for my friend Sunny ever since. I was living in her little doublewide on the outskirts of Battle Lake, Minnesota, and there was a strange man in her bed. My bed.

I flicked on the cat-shaped lamp and angled the lit ears toward the intruder still sprawled on top of the handmade Amish quilt I had lucked on in the Fergus Falls Salvation Army. I yanked it from under him and covered up my body, clad in only my summer pajamas—an oversized, threadbare white tank top. I was usually comfortable with my five-foot-six, 140-pound frame, but I wasn't a flasher. I pulled my disheveled hair away from my face and stared down my pointy nose at the relaxed drunk.

"Sunny isn't here." I was hoping to conjure a verbal vanishing potion, but my heart was still pummeling my rib cage, and my voice shook. Sunny's dog, Luna, now my foster dog, barked from outside the open window. "Who are you?"

"Mira?"

I squinted. Happy Hands knew me, and his voice scratched an itch in the back of my memory. "Jason?"

"Yeah. You're not Sunny." He sounded bored.

Yup, it was Jason. I had met him through my moody friend C.C. ten years earlier, when my hair was dyed black, I smoked clove cigarettes, and dark, flowing clothes were my signature. Thank God for evolution.

Back then, C.C. and I were both awed freshman trying to act like we weren't scared by the vastness of the U of M and its forty-thousand-plus students. We had ended up as dorm mates through the luck of the draw, two small-town girls, and hit it off from the word go. She brought me to her hometown of Battle Lake on Thanksgiving break of our first year. A few months later, I introduced her to the guy who gave her genital warts, so I suppose, looking back, we're even.

During that first introduction to Battle Lake, I met Sunny, one of C.C.'s close friends. I also met Jason Blunt, a high school classmate of theirs. I knew him from the parties C.C. and I would road-trip to during college breaks, but he and I never really connected. He was the guy always trying to get in everyone's pants, the one who tried to marry anyone not dumb enough to sleep with him.

He was tall, over six feet, with dark hair and dark eyes, cute in a way that would be hot if he were an actor but that ended up just average since he was a perpetually horny fiber-optic-cable layer. In small-town tradition, Sunny and Jason had slept together in high school, as had most of their friends. Musical beds. I suppose the process evolved out of long winters and bad TV reception.

I hadn't seen Jason in over five years. Word was he had to relocate to Texas to find a woman to marry him since every woman in Minnesota had turned him down. Apparently he hadn't gotten the news that Sunny had moved to Alaska for the summer, and he was making his area horn call.

"What're you doing back in Battle Lake?" I asked. I felt light-headed and ill. It occurred to me that maybe Otter Tail County had some sort of magnetic pull on people who entered it. That's the only way to explain why I was still here, running the library and writing for the local newspaper, after the last month I had lived through. It's a long story, but the short version is that I had just started falling for a guy when I found him shot through the head in my library a couple days later.

When I had first met Jeff, I was impressed with his maturity and character. After he was shot and left there for me to find, I learned again the harsh truth that how I feel about someone has no effect on whether they get to live or die. I thought I had learned that one well enough when my dad died in a car accident the summer of my junior year in high school, but in my experience, life keeps dragging you back to the same table until you pick the right food. Anyhow, the whole Jeff Wilson ordeal taught me the mental benefits of tying up loose ends. I also turned twenty-nine last month, but that milestone got lost in the shuffle.

Jason sat up and rubbed a red scrape on his shoulder, his back to me. He had put on about forty pounds since I last saw him, and I couldn't help but notice that he had stripped down to his faded black boxers. Confident guy. "I'm in town to visit the 'rents. Got anything to eat?"

My mouth opened in a yell, but he was out of bed and in the kitchen before I could answer. Apparently, if he wasn't getting laid, he was getting fed. I squelched the urge to hand him a mirror. I had just seen a show on chimpanzee behavior on the Nature Channel and was pretty sure the shiny glass would keep him busy for hours. No, better to get rid of him. As I grabbed for my robe, I hissed at the part of me that was thinking like a schoolgirl, worried that he would get mad at me if I was rude to him when I knew I should be kicking the trespassing bastard out on his ass. Media conditioning is a bitch.

I looked around my bedroom for a pair of shorts to pull on under the robe. The wrought-iron bed was stripped down to its sheets, and I grabbed the quilt off the floor and tossed it on top. I discovered the cutoffs I had been wearing earlier today underneath and tugged them on.

Now that I was no longer terrified by an intruder in my bed, I could not ignore a black memory that was squirming its way into my consciousness. I didn't want to be overwhelmed by the remembering, but I couldn't sit on it any longer, not now that we were bathed in light and I could hear him making himself comfortable in my kitchen.

It was born several years ago, that black memory, the summer before C.C. and I graduated from college. The night had opened with promise—a bonfire by the lake, a keg of Leinenkugel's, and a CD player hooked up to someone's car lighter. I remember feeling pretty that night, and excited to be with friends.

Jason was there, and it wasn't long before he hit on me. His hair was longer then, shiny black and curling around his shoulders. He leaned in to tell me a joke, and his wide grin was flirtatious. He really was cute. I was flattered by the male attention but not drunk enough to latch on to the token male slut so early in the evening. When I didn't bite, he moved on to the next chick, and I forgot about him. He hadn't forgotten about me.

When I walked into the woods to pee, he followed me quietly. He waited until my pants were down to push me back, onto the ground, and cover my mouth with his fist. His hand smelled musty, like composting leaves.

I heard Sunny call my name at the same moment the zip of Jason's pants cut through his fumbled grunting. He jumped off me when Sunny appeared and then staggered back to the party. She was weaving and giggling like we were playing hide-and-go-seek and didn't stop him when he shoved past her. Though she helped clean me off, she didn't have much sympathy for my situation. She wanted to keep the good times rolling and said he was just drunk and had misinterpreted my interest. She seemed mildly offended that I would even consider that a good friend of hers could be a potential rapist. I started to wonder if maybe I had overreacted.

I saw Sunny laughing with Jason later that night as I sat on the fringes of the party and tried to act normal, chain-smoking so I'd have an excuse to keep my hand in front of my swollen mouth. I still don't know what was more of a betrayal—Jason's aggression or Sunny's lack of support for me.

In the way of small-town German descendants, however, we never talked about that bad night again. Life went on, and when I ran into Jason, he was distant and vaguely unpleasant. Everyone else treated him like a lovable goofball, though I did notice that some people made a point to steer clear of him. Myself, I got to a place where I either wondered whether I had imagined the whole thing or thought that maybe he had been too drunk to remember his attack on me.

Despite the passage of time and my own self-doubt, it was still impossible to feel comfortable with him in my house, but I didn't want to work myself into a panic attack, either. I rationalized that there were plenty of people who liked Jason, and he did have a good sense of humor. I stopped just sort of making excuses for his past behavior and strode purposefully into the kitchen.

The doublewide was set up so that I had to walk past the front door and through the living room to get to the open kitchen, a Formica-topped counter creating the only separation between the two rooms. The living room was decorated in Early Cabin, including a secondhand rust-colored couch, cinder-block and wood-plank bookshelves, mismatched lamps, and a 1984 RCA color TV sporting tinfoil-hugged rabbit ears. The floor was carpeted in forest green, except for the pale green spots where the sun hit it regularly.

The kitchen was nicer. It had come with all new appliances, including a dishwasher, when Sunny purchased it. A U-shaped countertop housing the stove and the sinks took up one half of the room. The other half was dominated by a glass-topped dinner table with four wicker chairs around it and also held some freestanding cupboards and a ficus plant. I had kept the kitchen pretty much as Sunny had left it, other than scrubbing it top to bottom, putting my pictures up on the fridge, and alphabetizing the spice rack.

"So, I bet your parents are happy to see you." With my thumbs, I was inscribing infinity symbols on the nails of my middle fingers. I shoved my hands into the pockets of my robe to hide the nervous habit.

"Haven't been there yet." He grabbed a pot from the particle-board cupboards and stuck his hand in the food cabinet all in one smooth move. "You're gonna need more Potato Buds."

I sucked in a deep mouthful of air in a trapped sort of way and sat down on a stool next to the island, girding myself for a confrontation. I knew from experience that it would be easier to get rid of him full than kick him out hungry, so I promised myself I would show him the door as soon as he was done eating. This was my house, and I wasn't going to let him intimidate me in it. At least not for longer than half an hour. I slowed my heartbeat, made a mental note of the objects within reaching distance that I could use as weapons if need be—the knife rack was inches away in the crook of the counter, and I could've touched the nearest lamp with my hand right then if I'd wanted to—and turned to look into the night.

The June evening was unusually warm, following the precedent set by May, and was soaked in the smell of fresh-cut grass and rich, black dirt. If I listened below the sounds of boiling water and clattering pans, I could hear mosquitoes whining. Whiskey Lake's waves lapped against the rim of its sheltered arm six hundred yards from my front door, and the oaks and elms stood still as stone, their fresh leaves hanging motionless and a little too green from the exhilaration of spring. I cocked my head. If there was no wind, there should be no waves. I stood and walked to the open door and peered through the screen. Sure enough, I caught the low hum of a motorboat on the far side of this offshoot of the lake. I looked at the clock hung by the door. It was 2:34 a.m.

"What's a boat doing out at this time of night, and with no lights on?" I whispered, my fingertips on the cool screen.

I jumped as Jason answered from directly behind my left shoulder. "Probably looking for the diamond. This lake'll be crawling by tomorrow."

TWO

WHEN SUNNY'S PARENTS HAD disappeared nearly twenty years earlier, all of their property had automatically gone to their only child. It came to a little over a hundred acres of the prettiest land in Minnesota, with a sky-blue farmhouse, a barn, and three red sheds planted in the center of it. The house had burned down a year ago and been replaced by a doublewide, but that only marginally affected the charm of the place. There were still rolling hills, tillable farmland, and wild prairie freckled with thick hardwood groves. And the jewel was the lakeshore. Sunny owned the whole side of Whiskey Lake from the public-access boat landing to the little private beach a mile north.

The only gap in her empire was the jutting arm of land known as Shangri-La Island. Technically, it was a mini-peninsula and not an island, since it wasn't completely surrounded by water. It shared the two-mile driveway that abutted Sunny's farm and wound east and then south onto the island. A good stretch of this isthmus of a driveway was waterlocked, with Sunny's pond on one side and Whiskey Lake on the other.

The dwellings on Shangri-La—a beautiful main lodge and four cabins for the help—were built in 1924 by Philadelphia millionaire Randolph Addams and his wife, Beatrice Carnegie, granddaughter of Andrew Carnegie. Addams had fallen in love with the area on a fishing trip and hired local workers to build the main structure out of fieldstone and cedar. Local legend had it that one summer a wealthy guest of the Addamses had gone swimming wearing a diamond necklace—a gold chain with a diamond dewdrop as big as a baby's fist dangling from it. She emerged from the water without the necklace, and the other guests and staff searched frantically. The jewel was never found.

According to Jason, that was about to change. A national travel magazine had published an article describing and rating the resort that now occupied Shangri-La Island. The article mentioned the missing diamond. Many people read the article, and one of those people was an editor at the *Star Tribune* in Minneapolis. She had family in the Battle Lake area and thought the missing diamond necklace would be an appealing human-interest story.

The front-page headline of the Friday, June 1, Source section read, "Hope for a Diamond in Minnesota's Gorgeous Lake Country." The paper planned to plant a fake diamond in a weighted box in the lake on Monday the fourth, and they were offering five thousand dollars and a free week at Shangri-La to whoever found it. Apparently, they did not have complete faith in the legend of the real diamond or, if they did, had decided it was beyond recovery. But the article made good copy and was a boon for the tourist industry that drives Minnesota summers.

Unfortunately, the paper had not seen fit to warn either the local papers or the residents of Battle Lake. Here I was, Mira James, star reporter (well, reporter at least) for the *Battle Lake Recall* and living on the very shores of Whiskey Lake, and I had to get the scoop from a guy who liked ketchup and Easy Cheese on his rehydrated mashed potatoes. Technically, it was Sunday morning, which meant the contest started tomorrow.

"So how'd *you* hear about it?" I asked peevishly.

Jason took a chug off the can of Dr. Pepper he had found in the back of the fridge and burped. I noticed he had avoided looking directly at me since I had shrieked at him bedside. His jaw had been clenched since he arrived, leaving a shadow from his temple to his mouth. His brown eyes traveled around the room, annoyed or distracted. He wasn't even close to a smile, so I couldn't see if he still had those brace-straightened whites that made girls' hearts flutter. Until they got to know him better, that is.

He turned to grab his shirt. He had folded it in a pile with his pants and shiny dock shoes outside my bedroom door, next to a flashlight and a six-pack of cheap beer. "Word gets around."

"All the way to Texas?"

His shoulder blades tensed. Although he hadn't minded talking about the diamond between shovelfuls of Potato Buds, when it came to discussing his life, he wasn't very forthcoming. He rubbed the scratch on his back again, this time with more intensity. It looked an angry and infected red in the light, and I could see two lighter scratches running parallel to it. I wondered if he was getting cat scratch fever. The kind you get from getting scratched by a really big cat. "I left Texas a while ago. I was working up on the East Coast."

"Doing what?" My fingers were still tracing infinity shapes. I ran my hand through my shoulder-length brown hair and forced my body to be still.

"Working." He pulled his shirt sharply over his head, covering the scratch marks. Suddenly, he couldn't leave fast enough.

"Mmm-hmm." Just like that, the power in the room shifted. I blinked at him, doubtless much like a pit bull does when it senses it should probably let go of the person in its mouth but can't remember how to unlock its jaw. "What kind of work?"

He stopped in mid-tuck and turned toward the door. "Construction."

"House or road?"

"Jesus, Mira, back off!"

My neck twitched in response to his tone of voice. He had more than blue balls on his mind. If I was reading this situation correctly, Sunny's house had been Jason's first stop. If he were really in town to visit his parents, then he would have already been to see them at least once. Horny or not, he was still a born-and-bred Minnesota Lutheran boy, and he knew his mom would never stop the nagging if she heard he had come to this house first.

No, there had to be more incentive to pull him over Sunny's way than the promise of Potato Buds and tuna surprise. The diamond was the obvious reason, but how had he found out about it? Jason didn't have a reputation as much of a reader, so it was unlikely he had heard about the missing jewel all the way over on the East Coast by perusing the travel magazine or the online version of the *Star Tribune*. And since no one in the Battle Lake area yet knew about the diamond search—because if they had it would have gotten back to the *Recall* given the momentum theory of

12

small-town words—it was even less likely that someone from here had contacted him. He was almost out the door, but I suddenly wanted him to stay and tell me how he had found out about the lost necklace contest and why he was so reluctant to tell me what he had been up to.

He brushed past me quickly, flashlight and beer in hand. His elbow connected with mine in a sharp crack, and I couldn't tell if it was intentional. At the door, he turned and glanced once into my eyes, his dark brown staring down my gray. And then the screen door slapped closed and I was left alone with a crusty potato-making pan, a counter full of open condiments, and the feeling that Jason and I would be seeing each other again really soon.

I wiped my nose and began cleaning up, not relaxing until I heard the roar of his car starting and could follow his taillights as they departed down the long driveway. My hands were still shaky, and I felt displaced and edgy. I knew one thing that would calm me down for sure, but I didn't like to give in to the bad habit.

I paced the kitchen, still thick with the smell of fake potatoes and Jason's spicy-cheap Drakkar cologne, and listed all the reasons it would be a bad idea to rip into my old standby: although it made me feel good for the moment, coming down was always hard; empty calories at night go straight to the designated ass pockets; and I'd need to brush my teeth again. *Screw it.* I walked to the freezer and pulled out a red and green Nut Goodie package quickly, before reason or good sense took over.

Frozen Nut Goodies are the only way to go in the summer. The cool chocolate slides around on your tongue, and the maple center gets hard and chewy all at once, like iced-up honey. I peeled the wrapper and bit off the chocolate lip, letting the sweet darkness and nuts merge in my mouth. When I reached the light brown maple center, I was forced to leverage the bar in the back of my mouth between the molars to crack off a piece. I braced a chunk and sucked it slowly, letting the crystallized, nutty sugar dissolve into my veins. I felt a spreading warmth as I settled into my Nut Goodie high, the world and all its creatures right for one perfect moment.

I let Luna in before I started cleaning. She usually slept in the house, but tonight, she had wanted to be outside, probably because of the commotion down at the lake. Had Luna been in the house, she would have woken me up before Jason got to my bed.

"Hey, girl. Wild night?" I asked as I scratched behind her ears. Luna was a German Shepherd mix that Sunny had found on the side of Highway 210 when she was just a puppy. When I took over as housesitter, the dog was part of the package. She got along fine with Tiger Pop, my calico kitty and consummate coward. I hadn't seen Tiger Pop since Jason had arrived, and my best guess was that he was sleeping in his second favorite spot in the house—the pile of clean clothes in the laundry room.

It was 3:23 Sunday morning by the time I had the kitchen cleaned, and a focused to-do list buzzed in my head: stop the presses and submit an article for Monday's *Recall* ASAP so we didn't look like dorks; ask around about Jason to satisfy my curiosity and get back my feeling of safety; get online and research the tale of Whiskey Lake and the real diamond necklace. Oh, and rent some diving equipment while there was still some to be had.

After the kitchen was in order, I forced myself to lie down and concentrate on the inside of my eyelids for two full hours. I considered it a major achievement that I only spent seventy-five per-

cent of that time considering that Jason Blunt was bringing nothing but bad luck with him and that maybe I wouldn't be lucky
enough to escape this time.

THREE

I woke up around seven a.m. Sunday with enough sand inside my eyes to make a pearl necklace. Two hours of worried sleep does not a pretty gal make. I threw off the quilt and vowed not to look in a mirror for at least twenty-four hours. A loon cried, sad and long, about two hundred yards from my bedroom window, and I looked out to see a low fog kissing the lake. The lake. I had to get to town and spread the word about the diamond contest on Whiskey Lake. I forwent a shower and instead slapped on some deodorant, pulled my hair into a twisted bun at the nape of my neck, and splashed cool water on my face and mint toothpaste on my teeth. I put Luna and Tiger Pop outside along with fresh water and full dishes of food, and I headed into town.

I drove through sleepy Battle Lake, the burg quiet but for a couple cars outside the Fortune Café—probably tourists loading up on gourmet coffee—and two heavy-duty pickup trucks pulling sleek, sparkly boats. Battle Lake is in what is called west central Minnesota. This part of the state is closer to the Dakotas than Wisconsin, near the pointy-elbow shape on the left side of the state when you're looking at a map. In the summer, the town swells with tourists who come in search of great fishing, quality beach time, comfort food at the local restaurants, and hiking at the state park right outside of the city limits. Locals grumble about the tourists, but Battle Lake would dry up without them. I had only been here since March, which put me somewhere between tourist and visiting-family-member status.

When I had first arrived in town, I got a job at the Battle Lake Public Library in addition to my newspaper job. I started out as an assistant librarian, but some freaky events in May had resulted in my being promoted to head librarian. This was good, not only for the slight pay bump but also because I didn't have a computer at home. Now that I was the boss of the library, I had regular access to the Internet.

I pulled into the empty library parking lot and chose a spot. The library was closed on Sundays, so I would be able to write uninterrupted. Once I got inside and fired up the computer, the article on the diamond didn't take too long to write. With a BA in English, not to mention a few graduate-level courses in the same, I was really good at plagiarizing. I simply downloaded a copy of the original *Star Tribune* article, wrote a new lead, reordered some words and replaced others, and the meat of it was complete. The problem was finding a way to make it seem like we had known about the diamond contest all along. As soon as a draft was complete, I tracked down the editor of the *Recall*, Ron Sims, at the paper's little headquarters in town to bring him up to speed.

When I walked into the office, the fresh, metallic tang of ink washed over me. Except for that smell, this two-room rented space could pass for a waiting area in the DMV. The walls were tan, and the carpet was tan with gray specks. There were no pictures on the walls, and the only furniture in the front room was Ron's desk, his chair, a filing cabinet, and a stack of the latest edition of the *Recall*. There was a Macintosh in the room at the rear, alongside the outdated but functioning printing press. I loved going back there. The press, with its humming, clanging parts, held so much potential, even though we just turned out small-town fare for the most part.

It took me all of thirty seconds to fill Ron in.

"Oh Christ," he said. "When did the *Star Tribune* article come out?"

Ron was a pretty harmless guy in his late forties. He had thinning gray hair and light brown eyes and usually wore tan clothes. In fact, he was the human version of his office. He was the owner, editor-in-chief, desktop publisher, full-time reporter, photographer, and salesman at the *Recall*, which was why he was in the office early on a Sunday. The newspaper was his main claim to fame, besides the fact that he and his wife had a tendency for excessive displays of affection, forcing them to do everything short of lift their legs and spray each other in public. The two of them had gotten kicked out of a bar or two for their extreme PDA, but mostly everybody in town was just happy to see married people making out with the people they had married.

Ron had originally hired me on to write fill-in articles, though he had recently given me more work since I broke the story on Jeff Wilson's murder last month. This included my very own recipe column, called "Battle Lake Bites." My weekly goal was to find some gastronomic combination that, in Ron's words, "was representative of Battle Lake." So far, my two hits had been Phony Abalone (chicken soaked in clam juice so it tastes like fish) and Deer Pie (think Freddy Krueger meets Bambi, and add Velveeta).

Between me and Betty Orrinson, who wrote the "Tittle Tattler," there were a total of three employees at the *Recall*. And unless Betty was holding out information, which would have been counterintuitive for her, not one of us had heard about the *Star Tribune* article until it was almost too late.

I slapped the downloaded copy of the *Star Tribune* article in front of him. "It came out June first. The contest officially starts tomorrow at dawn, but there were already boats out on Whiskey around two-thirty this morning."

Ron leaned back in his swivel chair, crossed his legs, and hoisted them onto his desk with a grunt, lacing his fingers behind his head. I imagine he was going for a Woodward and Bernstein pose of urgent journalistic thoughtfulness, but the gap in his shirt above the top snap of his pants leaked out too much belly-button hair to permit that.

"Damn big-city newspapers. Think they don't need to tell the little guy what's going on. Well, this little guy has a trump card."

I was thinking that this little guy looked like he had eaten a couple other little guys, but I didn't want to sidetrack his train of thought.

"We have something they don't have. We've got the human-interest angle. You know Shirly Tolverson, down at the Senior Sunset?"

I hadn't been around town long enough to know all the locals by name, but I certainly knew the Senior Sunset. In fact, I was becoming a little too familiar with it. It was a nursing home in the purest sense of the phrase, and I had spent a lot of time there when

I was investigating Jeff's murder, supposedly for my article in the *Recall*, but mostly for peace of mind. Actually, most of the residents there were great when they weren't looking for help breaking out. In fact, I had gone back just last week to help them till up and plant their little rectangle of garden, staying to play three-handed Schafkopf with some residents. I left $4.75 poorer and convinced I would spend more time there if not for the smell of the place. It was the perfume of a small-town prom gone bad—cafeteria food, cheap makeup, and Lysol. "I'm sure I could find her," I told Ron.

"Him. His dad sold the lumber to the Addamses to build Shangri-La, and Shirly helped out when he was a kid. I used to hear him tell tales of it at the Turtle Stew. Go see him pronto and find an angle. I'll pull the layout and make room." Ron hitched his pants and sat forward in his desk, a rare look of purpose in his eyes. "You e-mail me an article before midnight tonight. Damn good thing this paper comes out on a Monday, or we'd be caught with our pants down."

I saw a forty-watt bulb switch on over Ron's head, and I wondered if his "pants down" comment gave him an idea of something new to try with his wife. When I left, he was muttering about the "fishing contest on the back page" and "pissed-off Lutherans." He could complain about the hassle of rearranging the layout on a paper ready to go to press, but I think he was secretly pleased to have a sense of urgency on the job. That's why most people go into journalism: to feel like they're breaking news and helping people. At the *Recall*, most of our reporting dealt with who was dining with whom, who had gotten arrested for what, and whose kids had gotten scholarships to where.

I stepped out into the cloudy June Sunday and looked at my watch. 10:33. Probably snack time at the Sunset, but if I hurried the four blocks, I could be there and gone before lunch was served. I wasn't sure what a room full of geriatric diners looked like, but I was willing to bet the sound stuck with a person for a while. I'd make this quick.

I was strolling past First National Bank on a shortcut to the Sunset when a barn swallow swooped down from its nest in the bank clock and dove at my head. The deal with the bank clock is that it's really old and ornate and beautiful, but only one side tells time correctly, and I swear the correct side alternates. Today, the side facing downtown said it was 10:34 and the side facing uptown said it was 7:20.

I was concentrating on these details to keep my mind off the fact that a bird swooping at one's head was bad luck. I have a fear-love relationship with birds: I'm afraid of their little winged lizardness, and they love it. I try to keep my bird feeders at home full to appease the bird gods and to keep them from smelling my fear, but this little brown barn swallow diving at me was telling me something, and it wasn't good. I wondered if it had something to do with me bringing Tiger Pop when I moved here, or if maybe the water in the bird bath outside my doublewide was stale.

"Mira? Y'all are sure up early on a Sunday. It's my good luck, sweetie!"

Aw shit. That's what the swallow was telling me. It was just trying to warn me that Kennie Rogers, mayor of Battle Lake, was around the corner. Maybe I'd have to rethink my view of birds. "Hi, Kennie. Actually, I'm usually up—"

"And did you get your hair cut? It's so flattering, that field-worker look. So natural. I wish I could pull it off." Kennie beamed at me, smoothing her frayed denim vest with her free hand. She must have greased the inside to squeeze into it, because her boobs were squished together into an enormous uni-breast with barely a crack in the top.

Her hair was coifed to frosted perfection, the curled ends crackling with Aqua Net. One errant spark and she'd go off like a rocket. Her makeup was applied with its usual putty-knife precision, her eyelids a glittery purple underneath the penciled black brow, dark lines of blush along each side of her nose to make it look thinner, her lips a bruised raspberry with a brown pencil line tracing a perfect pout well outside her mouth's natural borders.

She was wearing rolled-up, faded Levi's and cork-heeled pumps, a la J. Lo, but instead of looking like a trendy Latina, Kennie managed to pass for a stuffed Norwegian. "Well, don't just stand there gapin' at me. Aren't y'all gonna ask me what's in my hand?" She waved a stack of papers at me.

"What's in your hand, Kennie?" I asked, remembering that one is supposed to pretend one's dead when approached by a charging animal.

"Flyers for my new business! Whee!"

Kennie's last business had been old-lady beauty contests, where there were no winners, if you know what I mean. Before that, it had been private house orgies for the aged, complete with bongs and naked rosemaling. I waved over Kennie's shoulder at an imaginary friend and took off jogging.

Kennie chased after me, quick as a cheetah in her strappy sandals, and grabbed my arm. "You silly! Just take a look. It don't cost nothin' to look." Kennie flashed me a sly smile.

I glanced around, my head twitchy, but church was in session and the streets were pretty empty. I was on my own, and I best take my medicine. "Let's see it, Kennie."

She smiled and nodded, eagerly handing over a brochure.

I turned over the folded paper. It looked like it had been produced with the cheap desktop publishing software that comes installed on most new computers nowadays. The paper was résumé-thickness, tri-folded to create a pamphlet. On the front were two clip-art suns, one next to the other, with the words "Minnesota Nice Inc." curved underneath like a grinning mouth. Held at arm's length, it looked like a New Age smiley face. I braced myself for wrinkly nudity of some sort and folded open the front flap.

"Well?" Kennie asked, balancing impatiently on one foot while she fiddled with her cheap metal ankle bracelet.

I glanced at her and then back to the first paragraph, which was actually a check-marked list:

✓ *Having trouble breaking up with that gal who doesn't let you watch football on Sundays?*

✓ *Can't kick that special someone off the funeral committee, even though NO ONE likes her five-meat hotdish?*

✓ *Don't want to tell Jimmy that he can't use your deer stand anymore because he's never got the hang of peeing out of a tree?*

I felt my inner head shake in disbelief as I read on:

Then Minnesota Nice Inc. is for you! We do your dirty work. The truth shall set you free, and we'll tell it for a fee!

I laughed. I couldn't help it. Kennie might finally be onto something. "So people hire you to tell the hard truth to someone for them?"

She nodded. "I knew you'd appreciate it, honey. Y'all and me are both intelligent women of the new millennium. We know we gotta do for ourselves."

She nudged me, hard, in the ribs, and grabbed her brochure back. "I'll give y'all one of these when I get some more printed. I'm sure you'll let me put a whole pack out at the library. Right, sugar?" Ah. The real reason for Kennie stopping me in the street. She smiled and waved her talons in my face, then turned on her five-inch sandal heels and tottered away.

I suppose a woman born, raised, and cured in Battle Lake who could pull off a Southern accent should be expected to surprise, but she still had caught me off guard. Minnesota Nice, indeed. I just wish I had written down the number. I'm not a big fan of confrontation.

Speaking of which, I hoped I could avoid one with the front-desk people at the Senior Sunset. It was sometimes hard to slip past the security door, depending on who was working. To me, it was just weird that the elderly had so little freedom. This place was like a minimum-security jail, except the inmates couldn't run to save their souls.

As I neared the main door of the Sunset, I thought about the turn of fate that had brought me here. Not just *here*, as in Battle Lake, but here at this point in my life. I had fled my tiny hometown of Paynesville as soon as I had my high school diploma in hand.

Minneapolis, one half of the Twin Cities, sang my siren song, and I started out in the dorms at the university and then set up base in my tiny loft apartment on the West Bank of the Mississippi. After ten years in the big city, though, I hadn't felt any more grounded or purposeful than I had in the horror known as high school. I had been bopping around grad school, waiting tables, and hoping someone would discover me and bring meaning to my life. To make matters worse, I had been cultivating a drinking habit rivaling my dad's.

I remember one particularly lost day, about five months before Sunny called to ask me to housesit in Battle Lake for her, when I was walking home from a late shift at the Vietnamese restaurant where I spent most of my waking hours. It was an icy November night, and I wore black Aerosoles, taupe knee-highs under black cotton pants, and a fish-sauce-splattered white shirt. I had forgotten to remove my required black bow tie, and the smells of spring rolls and curry swarmed between my head and the cold air like sluggish bees.

It was ten-thirty, two and a half hours before bar close, and I felt relatively safe. Even when I noticed the man walking across the Washington Avenue bridge twenty paces behind me, I didn't think much of it. The streets were well lit, but out of habit I crossed to get away from the stranger. He crossed shortly behind me. I crossed back. He followed. I was about two blocks from my apartment, and I could see a clot of people laughing and living outside of Bullwinkle's, a local bar. If I could get past the empty corner I was nearing, I would be enclosed in the warm light of their company and safe from the man who was following me.

I wasn't going to run. I was going to walk steadily. My gloved hand felt for my apartment keys deep in my pocket, and I laced one between each of my knuckles. I could hear the man coming closer, his breath matching mine, his feet crunching on the layers of ice frosting the sidewalk like a cake. Forty feet in front of me, I could see the Bullwinkle's group. Traffic buzzed past, everyone encapsulated in their protected, cozy cars. Suddenly, the man grabbed my shoulder and twisted me around to face him. He wore a woolen cap pulled low over his face, and he brushed up against me, something hard pressing against my side. I felt a hand inside my coat, and then a sharp tug at my shoulder, and then he was gone, empty-handed. I didn't know if I had been molested, almost robbed, or hugged.

It happened so quickly that I didn't take my hand or my keys out of my pocket. I just watched him run away. Later that night, I lay in bed thinking about this life I had chosen for myself, in which I worked, slept, and drank, with only the occasional failed mugging to break up the monotony. It didn't fit. Fast-forward six months, and here I was, in Hamm's beer's land of sky-blue waters, one dead lover under my belt and becoming a regular at the local nursing home. Was this life better than random pat-downs by strangers?

I stepped off the sidewalk and crossed the street toward the landscaped front lawn of the Senior Sunset. Battle Lake had one main drag—Lake Street—with various avenues leading off of it like fish ribs off a spine. The Sunset was on one of the back streets, around where the dorsal fin would be. The area was mostly residential, and the houses were small and boxy, built in the fifties. It was quiet back here, except for the random ringing of church bells, and when a breeze picked up, it carried the smell of fresh-baked bread. I started to pull open the Senior Sunset lobby doors when I heard a "Psst!" from the bushes.

I swiveled my head to the right and spotted a fuzz of light gray and apricot on the other side of the yellow-flowered potentilla bush. "I can get you a pack of cigarettes, mint-flavored Maalox, or a pretty new crossword book," whispered the voice.

"Mrs. Berns?" Mrs. Berns was one of the younger residents, a spitfire who pretty much came and went as she pleased. My overriding hope in life was to have as much spirit as her in my golden years. And maybe to have her sex life, though I'd be okay with that kicking in anytime soon. This woman had more moves in one arthritic pinky than I possessed in my whole body. She claimed it took her nine marriages to figure out that she didn't need to buy the cow to get the milk, and she'd been burning up the geriatric singles scene in Battle Lake ever since.

I walked over the stone path and peered behind the bush. Mrs. Berns was perched on a three-legged gardening stool, an inventory list in one hand and a short library pencil in the other. Her hair covered her head like a steel-wool hat, and most of her face was lost behind a pair of enormous square-framed sunglasses. "Did you just have eye surgery, Mrs. Berns?"

"Ssshh!" she hissed. "Whaddya need? Liquor? Betty Page poster? *Perry Como's Greatest Hits*? You name it, I can get it."

You know, as weird as it was, I had to admire the entrepreneurial spirit of this town's women. "Mrs. Berns, I can buy all that stuff out here. I'm going *into* the nursing home. You should sell to the people who can't get *out* of the nursing home."

She looked down at her check-free inventory list and back at the front door, and back at her list again. "Damn!" She grabbed her stool and whipped past me, leaving a faint smell of lemon verbena and pressed face powder.

I followed her into the nursing home and was greeted by a wall of odor—antiseptic, fear, and something a little too sweet to pinpoint. The sweet smell actually was reminiscent of marijuana, but I wasn't going there. I had already encountered the passion for pot held by a certain sector of Battle Lake's geriatria, but I saw no gain in acknowledging it.

The Senior Sunset was set up like a cross between a dorm and a hospital. The floors were shiny, faux-marble linoleum, and the walls were institutional green. The pictures hung on the walls looked like the work of a four-year-old with watercolors, all of them set in brass frames exactly five feet off the ground. I suppose the blended pastel colors were meant to soothe the clientele into forgetting they were reasoning, functioning human beings. Thank God that Mrs. Berns was doing her part to keep the resistance alive.

The ceiling was covered with those squares of pocked ceiling tiles that can be found in any high school. They did wonders for the acoustics, which presently were being tested by a Muzak version of Blondie's "Rapture" piped out just loud enough to be annoying. I walked to the front desk like a woman in charge.

"What room is Shirly Tolverson in, please?" I could hear a faint crying in the distance, and the bilious sound of Judge Judy on a bender piping out from the community room.

The man-child behind the counter wore two-toned beige sunglasses, an unruly mop of Prince Valiant–styled brown hair, and a tie-dyed, long-sleeved Metallica shirt peeking out from under his janitor scrubs. He held a mop in one hand and tucked the phone under his ear with the other. "Yeah, down the hall, fifth door on the right." He waved me on and returned to his phone conversation.

I almost signed in before realizing that I might not be allowed to enter if I was still standing here when the receptionist, who must have been on break, returned. I really didn't have a legitimate reason to be at the Sunset, though I could have lied if necessary. I scurried down the hall and slipped into the fifth door on the right. Mr. Tolverson was lying on the bed, a carpentry book in one hand, *Jeopardy* on TV, and a bowl of peanut M&M's within reach. I liked this guy's priorities.

"Mr. Tolverson?"

He glanced over at me, pulling his trifocals farther down his nose. Unlike most residents of the home, who wore white "convenience clothes," he was dressed in street attire—ironed khakis and a plain white T-shirt. His hair was a crisp white and thick as a dictionary. The brown of his eyes was watery but still sharp, and his lips showcased a smile of even white teeth. They were probably dentures, but who was I to judge? He was a hottie of an old guy.

"May I help you?"

"Mr. Tolverson, my name is Mira James. I'm a reporter at the *Battle Lake Recall*."

"Oh yes, of course. I read your article on Jeff Wilson. A true shame about him. What can I do for you?"

I considered embellishing my story so we didn't look so stupid at the *Recall*, but Shirly Tolverson didn't seem like a man to lie to. "Ron Sims sent me over. We got scooped by the *Star Tribune*. Apparently there was a diamond necklace lost a number of years ago at Shangri-La, and Ron thinks you might know something about it. I'm trying to write a human-interest angle on the same story."

Shirly set his book down, took off his wire-rimmed glasses, and rubbed his eyes. He sighed profoundly. "What's the sudden interest in the diamond?"

I studied him. The mention of the necklace hadn't piqued his curiosity; it had tired him. "The *Star Tribune* is running a contest. The first person to find a decoy box in the lake gets five thousand dollars. They don't have any hope of finding the original lost diamond, I don't think. It's mostly a marketing article for the tourism industry around here."

Shirly got a distant look in his eye and leaned back on his pillow. "Shangri-La, located in the mountains of the Blue Moon." The reference was lost on me, but I didn't want to seem stupid so I kept that to myself.

He looked in my direction, a little past my head and to the left. "Well, Mira James, pull up a chair and I'll tell you what I know. When I'm done, you can decide for yourself if this necklace is something worth finding."

FOUR

TURNS OUT SHIRLY TOLVERSON had been a gofer for his dad back in the twenties when Shangri-La had been built. One spring afternoon, Randolph Addams had sauntered into Tolverson's Lumber and told the senior Mr. Tolverson that he wanted to build "a little cabin" down on Whiskey Lake. First, he bought the peninsula and access to it from Sunny's great-grandfather. Then, the road out to the six acres that was really a wide spot on the isthmus needed to be built. Next, the builders constructed several outbuildings and four servants' cabins.

When it came time to build the main lodge, no expense had been spared. The architect ordered Otter Tail County fieldstone to craft the foundation, supporting pillars, and fireplaces. Mr. Addams sent for Brazilian mahogany beams all the way from South America. The porch window frames featured out-swinging sashes, grooved and cut for both screens and shutters with all the hardware concealed. The workers finished the outside with stained cedar shakes.

Once the main structure was completed, the architect ordered hand-cut French stained glass to fill in the doors leading from the large living room to the wraparound porch. He also had a system of buzzers installed all around the interior that connected to the servants' cabins and had a dumbwaiter set up so food could travel from the first-story kitchen to the second-story rooms without being seen.

The Addamses hosted grand parties for their friends from the East once Shangri-La was completed. Randolph Addams's associates would stay in the main lodge and be catered to by the servants, who resided in the cabins. Not all the workers were live-ins, though; Addams hired on Shirly to do lawn work and run odd errands for the household. He'd been on the beach the day the necklace was lost, working as a towel boy.

"So you saw the woman lose the necklace?" I asked.

"In a manner of speaking." Shirly pulled his glasses off and rubbed his eyes. "I saw her go into the water with a diamond the size of a caramel around her neck. I saw her walk out of the water without it."

I smiled. "Are you being intentionally vague?"

"Vague isn't the word, Ms. James. Her necklace wasn't the first piece of jewelry to disappear that summer, though that diamond necklace was the official end of the relaxed days at Shangri-La. She put up quite a stink when she lost it—made us workers search on hands and knees in two feet of water for three days. She swore she was going to make Mr. Addams replace the necklace if we didn't find it." Shirly studied the back of his veined hands. "Tell the truth, I don't know if she didn't *plan* to lose that necklace."

"Why would she do that?"

"She came from an upper-class East Coast family. The Krupps, I believe, was the family name, from New York State. Back then, it took a lot longer to cross the country, so you remembered when someone came from New York or California.

"She never seemed to have as much money as the other guests, and she seemed angry about it. One day, I caught her upstairs in Mr. and Mrs. Addams's bedroom, over in their closet. She was scared, and then angry when she saw it was just me. I think she was hiding something back there, and she didn't want anyone else to know about it.

"Later that day, she loses her necklace, and it's me who's searching for it. When I couldn't find it, she made Mr. Addams fire me and any leftover part-timers who had built the place. She said we were a bunch of lazy thieves."

"If she lost it herself, why would she accuse you guys of being thieves?"

Shirly winked at me. "My guess is she had something to hide herself. Or maybe we reminded her too much of herself. Rumor had it that she was dirt poor until she married Mr. Krupps. It wasn't but a couple months after she had us fired that Mr. and Mrs. Addams sold the property, only a handful of years after they built it. They were sick of dealing with all the thievery that was going on and all the police questioning that came with it. Shangri-La's been a resort ever since."

"Was it a real diamond necklace that she lost?"

"She claimed it was."

He clearly did not want to go on the record about that, but I got the impression the only real thing about that necklace was the bad luck it brought Shirly. I vowed to find out the whole story, even if

I had to track down one of the original Addams family members. Ha. The Addams family. I leaned back in my chair, just now noticing that my butt was asleep. "That's quite a story, Mr. Tolverson. Mind if I use it all in the article?"

"Not one bit," he said, smiling at me. "Peanut M&M?"

On my way out, I was contemplating how many years older than me Shirly Tolverson was. At twenty-nine, I was becoming more open to dating outside my generation. I feared I was close to, if not immersed in, the relationship-atrophy phase of my life. It was a stage I'd seen coming for a while, a place in my personal evolution where if a guy hadn't gotten here with me, he'd be reluctant to leave the comfort of his train to jump on mine. Call it the "What do you mean you don't like peas in your macaroni and cheese?" point that we all reach, where we are too set in our ways to realistically expect a healthy relationship with another human being.

The threat of this specter was forcing me to consider new dating realms, though so soon after Jeff's death, I was officially gunshy about men from now until the end of the time. The male of the species had a lot to offer in theory, but in my experience, they had a tendency to die too soon. Not to mention that my last official date was with a professor from a local college who turned out to be a post-operative transsexual. My "friend" Gina had found him for me online, and in her defense, his online thumbnail had been cute. After our first lunch date, I knew something was a little off, but I thought it was me. Turns out it was him.

My dad was another example of what could go wrong with men. He had been an interesting man, a career alcoholic too smart for his own good. My childhood was a tapestry of forced normalcy punctuated by raucous fights between my parents. By the time I was seven, I knew I couldn't have friends over because if my dad wasn't drunk, my mom would be yelling at him for being drunk the day before. I spent a lot of time in my room with my imaginary friends. It wasn't all bad—my family traveled a lot in the summer in the car, and when dad was in public, he would usually stay sober. And even drunk, he wasn't mean, just crazy. He believed he could control the wind and speak French. Apparently, both wind-talk and French share a lot of root words with pig Latin.

By my teen years, I'd learned how to shut down my emotions so I wasn't a forced passenger on his roller coaster. I got even better at that after he died the summer before my senior year. He was driving drunk and slammed head-on into another car when he swerved over the center line. He killed himself and a passenger and her baby in the other car. I finished growing up that day. I still wasn't sure if that meant I became an adult or a permanently stunted child. Actually, I wasn't so sure there was a big difference.

I was so lost in thought on my way out of the Sunset that I was on the other side of the security doors and all the way to the lobby before I noticed the crowd. I stood on my tippytoes to see what was going on. In the center of an elderly mob was what appeared to be a Harlequin clown and a lion tamer accompanied by a small person dressed as a lion.

"How about you, young lady?" boomed the lion tamer, beckoning to me dramatically. "Wouldn't you like to see a local production of the honorable William S. Shakespeare's *The Taming of the Shrew*, starring esteemed members of your community and played out in a Gothic carnival setting?"

I stepped back as he stepped forward, shoving a piece of paper into my hand. I looked at him, confused. Had any of my English profs ever mentioned Shakespeare's middle name? I decided they hadn't and made a mental note to check out whether or not it was really an *S*. And what was going on?

I glanced at the second leaflet of the day to be shoved into my hand. It was card stock with gilded letters in a flowing serif font proclaiming, "The Famed Romanov Traveling Theater Troupe Is Coming to YOUR Town!" Underneath were pictures of the selfsame lion tamer, the Harlequin clown, comedy and tragedy, and various scantily clad Gypsy harlots. It was like the Renaissance Festival minus the big turkey legs and Dungeons and Dragons geeks. I wondered if Kennie was going to love this or hate it. I also wondered if the troupe knew the Senior Sunset folks were on lockdown. The rules, probably dictated by the Sunset's insurance policy, said the residents could only leave the premises if checked out by family. There was going to be no Gothic carnival for them, but I was intrigued.

"Sure," I said. I shoved the flyer back at him and studied his face. He wore the wide, empty grin of somebody who smiles for a living. His nose was broad, and his eyes, small and close set, darted around the room even as he talked at me. He seemed in habitual need of an audience. The Harlequin clown and lion wove in and out of the crowds, singing, dancing, and huzzahing, and I couldn't get a good look at either of them.

"'Sure,' it is! We are in agreement!" The lion tamer made a departing grand gesture with his plastic mini-whip and strode purposefully out the front doors of the Sunset, the clown and lion dragging along behind him, their backs to me. I looked around at the stunned room of nursing assistants and old folks. A familiar face came forward, shaking his head.

"And they call *me* crazy?"

"Hey, Curtis. How's the fishing?" Curtis Poling was another of my faves at the raisin ranch. People said he was crazy because he fished off the roof of the Sunset around lunchtime every day. The crazy part was that the closest body of water was a quarter mile away. I had found Curtis to be harmless myself, and he had a wicked smart streak that most people overlooked because he was old. He was also a hit with the ladies, due to his ice-blue eyes and rakish charm.

"Hmm, not so good. I might need to switch bait," he said.

I shook my head knowingly. "That'll happen." Truth was, I didn't eat fish and knew nothing about fishing. I had a rule about consuming anything that spent its whole life wet.

"Yup. Don't be a stranger." Curtis slapped me once on the butt and walked away.

It was time to go rent a diving suit and tank. I had already had too much human interaction for one day. As I stepped outside the home, the sun broke free from the clouds for the first time that day and warmed me to my toenails.

FIVE

THE ONLY PLACE TO rent scuba equipment in all of Otter Tail County is a little business called the Last Resort. The Last Resort has seven two-bedroom cabins, all carved out of the same country-schoolhouse theme. Every one of them has chipping white paint and pine green trim with screened-in porches on the front, and they all line up in a row to face the sandy brown beach of West Battle Lake. Each front porch holds a splintery picnic table next to a rusted Weber grill. The owners, Sal and Bill Heike, place a complimentary can of pine-scented Off! in every kitchen. To the far side of the seventh cabin is a fish-cleaning shed with running water inside and a scale-and-gut hole outside. Closer to the main road, Highway 78, is the Heikes' house, with the front office attached.

If you stay a full week at the Last Resort, you can rent a fishing boat with a ten-horsepower Evinrude for a hundred dollars. The bait is not included, though you can buy that and more at the store attached to the front office. The leeches and worms are in the same refrigerator as the vanilla Cokes, cheese, and bologna.

Years ago, Sal and Bill taught scuba certification as a side business. There was a train car intentionally sunk about two hundred feet straight out from cabin number three, and the scuba crowd brought in extra business. Unfortunately, pesticides and waste ponds around the lake had upset the delicate balance in the water, and now the weeds were so thick on this side of the lake that underwater visibility was only seven feet.

The Heikes kept the equipment, because used scuba gear doesn't go for much. Bill also kept the tank filler, though he always complained that it didn't pay, what with the cost of insurance. I knew the couple from around town, mostly from their frequent trips to the library to check out books on building your own greenhouse, making your own paper, growing your own organic vegetables, creating your own compost pile, et cetera. I also knew their twenty-two-year-old son, Jedediah. He had tried to sell me pot on several occasions, and every time, he was genuinely astonished that I declined. The beauty of having a brain-atrophying drug habit is that the world is born anew for you every day.

When I pulled my brown 1984 Toyota Corolla into the circle drive that marked the front of the Last Resort, it was Jed who limped out to greet me. "Hello, you! What can I do for you?"

I smiled at his excitement as I pulled myself out of the car. "What happened to your leg?"

Jed grinned sweetly, stretching the bong-shaped ring of acne around his mouth. "I twisted my ankle unloading a boat yesterday. I am so cool though, Mira. It's a beautiful day!" He waved his hands expansively in the June air, the sun shining down on his curly light-brown hair and through the spindly Fu Manchu mustache he was trying to grow. He hugged me spontaneously, and I let him.

When he stepped back, grinning, I returned his smile. He certainly made cluelessness look appealing. "Say, you wouldn't have any scuba equipment left to rent, would you?"

Jed actually scratched his head. "You know, weirdest thing. Everyone and her brother suddenly wants to rent our stuff. We're out."

My heart sank. I should have known. To be honest, I liked the idea of breaking this diamond story wide open, but the real reason I was going to so much trouble is I wanted the five thousand bucks for finding it. Since I didn't have any house payments and my electric bill was currently low, my only major expense was student loans—$276 every month. However, my part-time reporting job and now full-time library job paid only a frog's hair above minimum wage, which didn't leave a lot of spare cash lying around. It would be nice to add to the $20 in my savings account.

"Well, 'cept for my stuff and my ma and pa's. You could borrow that, if you like. We haven't been diving in a while."

"Jed!" I said happily. I was back on. "That would be great!"

He nodded his head like a happy Muppet and grabbed my hand. "Let's go back and check it out. It's all stored off the front office."

When we walked past the row of cabins and close to the store, I saw the Swenson's Landscaping truck around the side of the Heikes' house, which was done in the same chipping white and green as the cabins. My heart took a little electric leap. "Swenson's here doing some landscaping?"

"Yup."

"Who's doing the work?"

"Johnny."

My electric leap turned into a full-blown charge. I had had a crush the size of a Mack truck on Johnny Leeson ever since I had bought a flat of annuals from him a few weeks earlier. He was not tall, maybe five-eleven, in his early to mid twenties, and he had thick, longish blonde hair. The Scandinavian-exchange-student look wasn't normally my physical type, but he was strong and lean, he had even white teeth, and he knew everything there was to know about gardening: when to plant your peas, how much water to give your corn, where to bury your tulip bulbs, how to fertilize your roses—if it could grow in dirt, Johnny could advise.

For me, there was something very erotic about a man with a green thumb. If he could coax blueberries to grow in low-alkaline soil, what could he do with a prematurely jaded woman on a Sealy Pillow-Top? Plus, he always smelled like fresh-cut grass, and his eyes were the color of a blue raspberry slushie. I was pretty sure he didn't know I had these lusty organic thoughts about him. He just saw me as the chick who bought a few seed packets every week. My crush felt safe and exciting at the same time, in a crazy-lady sort of way. I told myself that I was being aloof and respectful in not hitting on him because he was currently dating Liza, personal stylist at the Under the Lilacs salon in downtown Battle Lake. The truth, though, was that I was a big hairy chickenshit.

"Where's Johnny now?" I said, my voice cracking slightly.

"Dunno."

"What exactly is he doing here?"

"Dunno."

By now we had reached the front office, and I didn't want to hurt Jed with any more probing. I could hunt around for Johnny on my own after Jed got me set up with the gear. I walked through

41

the creaky screen door he held open and glanced around the musty porch. The mildewy smell reminded me of my grandma's basement, a dirt-floor affair where she kept her canned goods. One corner of the porch was cluttered with cracked chairs stacked seat on seat, retired ice augers, and bright orange, foamy flotation devices. There were some old BCs—the buoyancy compensator vests that controlled a diver's depth and held the tank, air hoses and regulator, and dive gauges—and wetsuits hanging on ceiling hooks in the other damp-looking corner.

The main office was on the other side of the porch. It was surprisingly modern, with tongue-and-groove knotty pine walls, a sitting area with *In Fisherman* magazines splayed around a Skittles-filled candy dish, and a long front counter. There was a newish Dell computer behind the desk hooked up to a scanner, printer, fax machine, and flat-screen monitor. I wondered how the Heikes could afford the new technology. It seemed like their resort was half empty most of the time now, and they had no other source of income that I was aware of. I thought the money would have been better spent on paint for the cabins, but maybe the computer saved time and helped them book reservations and advertise.

"Just lemme check something real quick." Jed slid over the counter with a practiced air and grabbed one of the walkie-talkies from next to the computer. "Breaker, breaker, this is Angel Eyes, come in. Over." Jed winked at me and started getting the giggles.

"What is it, Jed?" Sal's voice was crackly.

"Heyah, Cool Momma, is cabin three still getting used tonight? Over."

Crackle. "No, Angel Eyes, cabin three canceled." Sal walked through the door, still speaking into the walkie-talkie. "They've moved to Shangri-La. Cool Momma out."

"Roger." Jed put the walkie-talkie back into its holder, and Sal clicked hers off.

"Hi, Mira. What brings you to our lonely resort?"

I pursed my lips. I genuinely liked the Heikes. Being ex-hippies, they passed for ethnic diversity in this town. "Business not so good, huh?"

"Not so good. But it'll pick up. We've got new plans."

I nodded at their computer. "You guys'll be fine. Anyhow, I'm just here to rent scuba equipment. I'm gonna do some diving on Whiskey."

"You and the rest of the world. What's going on over at Shangri-La?"

I considered not telling, but the world was going to know soon enough. I explained the missing-diamond story, the *Star Tribune* drop box, and the five-grand reward, adding, "I'm going to check it out. Who knows, maybe they put the box in early."

"Hmm. It might be time to pull me and Bill's gear out of retirement. Maybe we'll see you on the wet side, Mira!" Sal stepped over to the computer, clicked in a few words, and then went out through the back door. Jed followed her and was out of sight.

I knew he'd remember that I was waiting soon enough, so I poked my head out the side window and looked around for Johnny. It wasn't too hard for my eyes to find him next to the fish-cleaning shed, what with the sun kissing his rippling, sweat-glistened, shirtless body and his thick hair curling around his ears and neck where it had gotten hot and wet. Except for the feed cap on his head where the wreath of olive leaves should have been, he was Apollo soaking in his own brilliance.

"Hey, Johnny, how's the day treating you?" I asked nonchalantly. And quietly. In my head. No way was I going to destroy this moment with my own brand of dorkism.

He was getting ready to plant marigolds around the shed. I knew the flats of flowers he was unloading from the back of the pickup couldn't have weighed more than five pounds each, but when he grasped one of them, his arm muscles flexed and the lean ropes of his back defined themselves. His dark Levi's hung below the waist of his boxers, the whiteness of his underwear contrasting nicely with the brown muscles of his back. When he turned, I couldn't see his eyes behind his dark sunglasses, but his full lips were closed tightly as he concentrated on his work.

Once he had all the flats out, he leaned over the side of the shed with a garden spade in hand. He dug down deeply, removing divots of earth, which he placed off to the side. Then he methodically and gently removed a marigold from its four-pack, placed it in the hole, held the earth clump over the flower, and shook the dirt loose from the sod. He repeated this for every flower. By the time he was halfway down the side of the shed, the hot sun was sending trickles of sweat down his back, through the soft valleys made by his lean hips, and into his shorts.

"Ready to go, Mira?"

I blushed and kept facing forward when I heard Jed's voice behind me, thanking God almighty that you can't see a woman's hard-on. I shook my head to coax some blood back to my brain and turned to look into Jed's friendly eyes.

"Oh, there's Johnny!" Jed pushed me aside. "Hey Johnny, Mira's looking for you!" He yelled and waved simultaneously, pointing over to where he had pushed me, out of Johnny's view. "Here she is!" He held my hand out the window and waved it. I peeked my head around the corner and smiled lamely. Johnny gave one brief wave, flashed a short, solemn smile, and strolled over.

"Hi, Mira."

I looked down at my shoes, certain that a movie reel of my impure thoughts was playing on the big screen above my head. "Hi, Johnny. What're you planting?"

He looked back over his shoulder. "Marigolds, mostly. Have you gotten a chance to plant the zinnias you bought last week?"

My blush returned. He remembered I had bought zinnias. Could it be that he thought about me as much as I thought about him? "Not yet. You've been too hot outside."

Johnny cocked his head. "Excuse me?"

My face turned purple, and my internal switch flipped to Loser. "*It. It* has been too hot outside. To, you know, plant. Well, you better get to work, right? And I have to get to work. Not work, so much. More like investigating, you know. Underwater. I'm like a detective fish, but I can walk, too."

Johnny nodded his head at me, a small smile playing at the corners of his mouth. "Okay. Catch ya later, Mira. Jed."

Jed nodded dopily, and I slid down the wall into a pit of shame. With Johnny out of sight, I was able to flip my switch off Loser and onto Self-Loather. Could I be more of a moron? But that man, that body, those hands. I sighed. I liked Johnny just as he was—that is, at a distance—but I would have to seriously consider unpacking my vibrator out of homage to him. I had retired it a few months earlier because I was concerned about overuse. It got to where I was having a Pavlovian response to the sound of any small electric motor. Even the buzz of a blender on liquefy could get me going. After watching Johnny garden, though, I made a mental note to dig out the pink kangaroo from the bottom of the closet. If I didn't take care of myself, I was going to do something silly like ask the guy out. "You got anything to drink, Jed?"

He peeked his head through the archway that led to the little resort store. "We do have Coca-Cola. Or do you want to buy some pot?"

I grabbed Jed's hand and pulled him back into the porch. "Forget it. I gotta get out of here. Which BC do I get?"

"That black one in back is mine." He pulled out one of the rickety chairs and dragged the buoyancy compensator vest down, tossing it over to me. Its hoses and gauges slapped around like octopus tentacles.

"This one is wet, Jed. I thought you three hadn't been diving for a while."

Jed put his hands up in a "Who can remember everything?" way and hunted around for the rest of the gear. He ferreted out a wetsuit, compass, diving knife, fins, mask, and snorkel for me, as well as a dive flag and an inner tube to strap the flag to so that all boats would know there was a diver down. Outside, Jed filled two air tanks and helped me carry them to my car. I was careful not to be caught ogling Johnny. Again.

Once my Toyota was loaded, I avoided Jed's farewell hug for fear that I would get sticky pheromones all over him. I couldn't resist asking one last question, though: "Is it expensive to get Johnny out to help landscape?"

Jed scratched his curly hair. "Not for us. He's doing it in trade for some work my dad did for Johnny's mom. If you want, I'll ask Johnny how much he charges."

"No!" I said, a little too loudly. Was it bad that, for a moment, I had seriously considered hiring a hot garden man to ogle from the comfort of my back porch? Probably, if only because I was broke. One more reason to find the fake diamond, I guess. I hopped in my Toyota and was off. With one hand on the wheel, I scratched at a nagging itch on my head, and my fingernails caught on a bump. Shit. It was a wood tick, and it was stuck. It must have snuck into my bed while I was sleeping.

I ripped it off of my head, hanging on tight while running it through the length of my hair so I wouldn't lose it before I pulled it free. It squirmed between my thumb and forefinger, a white piece of my scalp stuck in its mouth and its tiny brown legs moving rhythmically. In lieu of a lighter to fry it, I punctured it with my thumbnail, leaving a half-moon shape on its tiny dark belly. I flicked it out the window as I pulled into my driveway. This was as close to hunting as I'd ever get.

I had decided to drive down to Sunny's little beach on the thick part of the road leading to Shangri-La. The spot was more grass than sand, but the lake was clear and hard-bottomed on this side, and it was quiet when the resort wasn't hopping. Today, the lake was peppered with boats, even more than on a usual Sunday, and I could see that the public lake-access parking lot was nearly full. I parked next to Sunny's beach, noting that most of the boats were concentrated on the east side of the lake, opposite Shangri-La. I wondered if they had found something.

The wetsuit and dive knife were easy to slip on, and a couple tugs set the facemask at the right pressure. The BC was old but functional, and I had it attached to the tank in under four minutes. I dragged the whole unit to the water so I could use the buoyancy of the vest to help ease the heavy tank onto my back. Soon, I was underwater, breathing in the silence of it.

Except for the Darth Vader sound of air leaving your mouthpiece, there is no perfect peace in this world like scuba diving. It has the safety and warmth of a womb once your wetsuit gets filled and warmed with your body temperature and you reach neutral buoyancy. Despite the weight of the tank, the sensory deprivation of diving elicits a rare sense of absolute freedom. I did a few horizontal twirls underwater, as I always do at the beginning of a dive. I actually had only been diving twenty or so times in my life, and only once in the ocean.

My father had learned how to dive in the service and taught me and my mom how when I was ten. We were at Daytona Beach, and it was winter, even in Florida. Dad talked a local dive shop into renting their gear, even though Mom and I weren't certified, with the promise that we would stay close to shore. There was no coral right off the beach and so nothing to see other than shady ocean. Still, the attention from my dad felt good, even if we were shivering together in slate-gray, fish-free water. A couple years later, he sprang for me to get certified, and we dived some of the lakes around Paynesville. I think diving was a way we could hang out together without having to talk, and I liked that Dad couldn't drink when we were doing it. Diving was something I still enjoyed but couldn't really afford.

This time was a freebie, though, and I was going to take pleasure in it. I tried to sneak up on a few perch, but they muddied the water and darted away like mercury. My hands were glove-free because I liked to play them through the scratchy weeds and loose silt on the bottom. I was careful not to get tangled in the line to my inner tube, to which was attached the red-and-white flag marking my dive. With all the boats on the lake today, I was going to stay close to the tube. I didn't need an Evinrude outboard all up in my grill. Once I felt acclimated to my environment, I settled in for some serious jewel hunting.

I found my bearings with my compass. I knew I was going to swim generally southeast, which would land me in front of the Shangri-La main lodge. I swam steadily, using my feet to power me, my hands streamlined at my side. I skimmed just above the weeds, glancing occasionally at the treasure troves of Hamm's cans and cut anchors that sprouted like anemones here and there.

For the most part, Whiskey Lake is a pristine, spring-fed lake with fifteen-foot-plus visibility on a good day, but even the cleanest lake has the remnants of fishers past. Actually, Whiskey Lake is what the locals call it. According to the DNR, who stock it annually with walleye fingerlings and yearlings, the real name of this body of water is Charter Lake. The lake itself is small, with a surface area of only 189 acres and a maximum depth of 46 feet. I had never dived in this lake before, but as a rule, I never went deeper than 30 feet when diving. It got too cold for me lower than that, though the bass, sunnies, and crappies that swarmed in the water without the DNR's help didn't seem to mind.

After ten minutes, I popped up to get my bearings. I was approximately forty feet from the Shangri-La beach, directly in front.

Good. Surprisingly, there didn't seem to be any divers in the immediate vicinity, though I counted seven boats dotting the far side of the small lake and I could see a group of divers ready to set off from the public access on the south side. I could hear their diving flag slapping at the wind.

I let myself slowly back down and continued to search around. It's hard to distinguish one chunk of lake bottom from another, but I thought I could get a feel for the area so I would know if anything had been changed or added. The *Star Tribune* box wouldn't be planted until tomorrow sometime, according to the article, and I wanted to get the lay of the land before then. A pile of white caught my eyes, and I kicked my way down. I checked my depth gauge. I was twenty-three feet below the surface and had over half my air left.

I scared up the bottom of the lake trying to draw close to the heap of white, and I had my face almost in the bones before I realized what they were. My throat constricted, and I took an involuntary breath through my nose, forcing the airless mask tighter to my face and giving me a temporary feeling of suffocation. I pulled back and put my hand on the dive knife strapped to my thigh, cursing the lack of peripheral vision afforded me by my dive mask. I tried to look around, but I felt like there was an enemy just out of eyesight. My agitated water stroking was making the atmosphere even murkier, and I forced myself to calm down. I could be on the surface in half a second by inflating my buoyancy compensator, and the pile of bones wasn't going to hurt me.

I floated back down a few feet and peered at the water burial, letting the silt and my pulse settle. I took my hand off my knife when I realized I was staring at a moose skeleton, all the parts laid cleanly on the floor of the lake as if the animal had drifted to the bottom in a last graceful ballet move to decompose peacefully. It looked like the whole set was complete and museum-ready. I was surprised. The bones had to have fallen recently, in the past winter or so, to be so clean and together, but I didn't think there had been moose in this area for years.

I filed the skeleton in my head as a good landmark for later and turned to swim back toward the beach I had set off from. The water was still slightly cloudy from my little fit by the bones, and I made haste to reach a clearer section. It took only five strong kicks through the shadowy water until I was on top of the human body clad in the shark-gray wetsuit, my tank tangled in the same rope that made and marked his grave.

SIX

I FOUGHT THE TWISTED rope like a hooked walleye, and the more I struggled to break free, the more I brought myself closer to the body jerking on one end of it like a rigid marionette. In one of my panicked gyrations, my eyes flashed onto the source of my present problem: a good-sized white rock at the bottom of the lake, a yellow polypropylene rope tied securely around it and leading to the sunken body and back around the oxygen tank on my back. But quickly that, too, was lost in the murk I was creating.

I couldn't fight the terror of drowning made real by the dead person who was almost on top of me now. My heart paused in my chest and built enough force to pound out my eardrums when it started again. I wrenched wildly to free myself, and the heavy, wet arm of the tangled body struck my head in a disjointed, dead swing and knocked my facemask off. I blinked once myopically, and only the rush of cold at my eyes let me know they were open. The water was as black and final as grave dirt, and I sucked in a nose full of it as a fear reflex. I was now completely blind, dancing with a corpse twenty-five feet underwater, and drowning.

When I got scuba certified, my instructor had spent half a day teaching us what to do if we lost our masks underwater. He hadn't covered what to do if we were also tangled in a rope tied to a rock and hooked to a dead body, but the principle was the same: stay calm and get to the surface. As I screamed for air and my lungs burned with water, I forced my raging fear instincts down and let the haunted corpse float right behind my unprotected neck. This allowed me to grab my BC vest buckles in a last-ditch effort to release myself and reach the surface. I wasn't deep enough to worry about the bends, even if I had been thinking that clearly. For now, my brain was waging a primitive battle between getting far, far away from the human carcass and getting to life-giving air.

I unclasped the first vest buckle as white bursts of light flashed behind my eyes, and I had the second one undone as everything began to go gray and my lungs blazed with the shapeless, crushing weight of inhaled lake water. I had been breathing liquid for several excruciating seconds, and my lungs were as full as a cement truck. My cold fingers struggled with the last black clasp, finally freeing it, and I kicked toward what I hoped was the surface. I felt myself blacking out even as I thrust forward, and I realized I no longer knew which way was up. I was disoriented from the underwater fight with the rope and body, and I had no air bubbles in my lungs to release and guide me, even if I could see.

I prayed that I was swimming toward the human world. If my head hit the soft bottom of the lake or just plowed through more water, I was dead. I had only a pinpoint of light left in my brain, and I wondered idly if my dad was waiting for me now. He'd been dead for over ten years, and I didn't know if I was ready to reconcile with him yet. With a few exceptions, he'd been a pretty selfish man when I knew him.

The one person I really wanted to see now was my mom. I had always loved her, but I had never trusted her, because she wasted so much time with my dad. I figured a smart woman would have gotten out early. His death pushed us even further apart. She certainly hadn't killed him, but she had kept herself and me strapped to the kamikaze plane that was his life. I wished more than anything to be able to go for a walk with her right now, smelling the perfume of summer flowers, feeling the breeze in the sweaty hairs stuck to my neck, and hearing gravel crunch under my feet. Instead, my world narrowed like that of a carnival goldfish in a sealed bag of water. The tiny circle of light in my brain grew brighter, and I remembered that my eyes were closed.

I opened them and saw a mirage of the sun reflected through a watery mirror, and I could almost feel its heat on my face. I reached out, and my hand brushed against something warm and soft. I grasped at it desperately, hungry to hold something solid. My hand slid off once, and I dug my nails in and pulled myself up.

I was welcomed by the glory of the warm sun on my water-soaked head as I clutched at my inner tube and surfaced weakly. I hung onto the side and vomited lake water and gasped for air, grateful for the providence that had brought me up near my life preserver. My whole body was trembling, but my mind was rejoicing. I was alive. I began to ineffectually kick for the shore. I wanted to get as far away from that dead body and its soggy grave as I could, and quickly. That could have been me. I had a feeling my exploratory diving days would be over for a while. Unless I knew exactly where that *Star Tribune* box was and dead bodies weren't, I wasn't going back in.

My childish kicks were bringing me away from the little stretch of beach I had started out on and closer to the public access, and soon the diving crew I had spotted earlier was beside me in their pontoon. I was dragged aboard, and I poured out my story between heaves. The dive crew untied their anchor, secured it to my inner tube as a marker, and took me ashore. They offered me an oversized Smurfs beach towel and a canteen of stale drinking water and told me they were from the Twin Cities, in Battle Lake to find the planted diamond. They had been scoping out the area when they saw me pop to the surface and start puking.

As their lukewarm water scraped down my raw throat and I absorbed the hot sun of an early June afternoon, my stomach growled, reminding me I hadn't eaten anything all day. In hindsight, that was good. I didn't want to feed the fishes, either with my body or its contents. It wasn't long before the Battle Lake police were on the scene, and the county water patrol arrived shortly thereafter.

It was time to tell my tale again, this time to thirty-eight-year-old Battle Lake Police Chief Gary Wohnt. Chief Wohnt had been on the Battle Lake force of two for over a year, and I had first met him when I'd discovered Jeff's body in the library in May. I had a paranoid feeling that he was going to blame me for this corpse.

There was no love lost between the Chief and me. He was thick-necked and bossy, given to bouts of adult acne, and had perpetually shiny lips. As a pure bonus, he had dark, inscrutable eyes and one of those ominously quiet personalities that forced me to fill the silence with embarrassing small talk and unrelated confessions. Plus, he had a weird thing with Kennie Rogers. The man knew I was always watching him out of the corner of my eye, and he returned the favor.

"Ms. James." His Frank "Ponch" Poncherello sunglasses made him appear impenetrable as he stood in front of me, one of his hips cocked higher than the other, his meaty hands hanging loose at his sides.

"Chief Wohnt." I was sitting on the open rear of a diver's Mitsubishi pickup, the Smurfs towel still held tight.

"Seems you were in the wrong place at the wrong time again."

"Seems so." Good thing I was too exhausted to stick my tongue out at him.

"Why don't you tell me what happened here? Don't leave out any details, even if you think they might be irrelevant."

He wrote down my story impassively, and there really wasn't much to it. I was diving, I got caught in a rope tied to a rock, and there was a dead body tied to the other end of the rope, floating free about ten feet from the surface of the lake. The Chief never asked me why I was diving in the first place, and I wondered if he already knew about the diamond necklace. He seemed to have an inside track on much of the town, possibly because of the off-hours "business ventures" he was rumored to have going with Kennie. I decided if he didn't know, I wasn't going to tell him.

He kept writing after I finished. When he finally snapped his notebook shut, he looked at me for twenty long seconds, his expression unreadable. "You shouldn't dive alone."

"I know. Can I go?"

"You can go, but don't stray too far from a phone. I might have more questions later."

The driver of the Mitsubishi offered me a ride home, and my still-shaky legs screamed at me to take it, but I was not going to relinquish the feeling of earth under my body, even if I had to crawl home. I said I would walk. It was less than two miles, and even though I was wearing a wetsuit and swim booties, it would be a welcome trek. The divers agreed to take the rest of my equipment back to the Last Resort, including the BC once it was retrieved.

Judging from the angle of the sun, it was pushing late afternoon. It truly was a beautiful day, and I had new appreciation for the warm June air and the buzz of the leopard frogs in the sloughs I was walking by on County Road 82. The tiny shock my muscles felt with each step on the pavement was ecstasy, and I smiled at the passing cars. I was alive, and I was on land.

My heartbeat revved up a little, and I actually whistled until it became too painful for my vomit-seared throat. I had shoved thoughts of my mother back into the detention room in my head that I saved for my family, and I was living life. Thirty minutes later, turning down my half-mile driveway, I contemplated the wisdom of a nap. I was mentally and physically bone-tired. I didn't want to close my eyes quite yet, though. I had looked at the inside of my eyelids enough for one day.

I found my feet leading me past the turn in the driveway that would have taken me to Sunny's, and before I knew it, I was at Sunny's little beach, where I had taken off on this dive a lifetime ago. I stripped off the wetsuit and booties, rolling my eyes at myself as I got to the dive knife strapped around my left thigh. I could have used it to cut the rope tying me to the lake bottom if I hadn't been so panic-stricken.

I slipped the shorts, T-shirt, and flip-flops that I had left on the shore over my swimsuit. Shading the sun from my eyes, I stared out at the to-do that was still happening on the lake. There were now two official-looking speedboats circling my inner tube, but I didn't see an ambulance at the access, and there was only one police car visible. That surprised me. I had learned last month that they always call in an ambulance, even if the body is dead. There must be another tragedy tying up the county ambulance elsewhere. The body I had found certainly could wait. I looked off to my right at the oak-shaded drive that led to Shangri-La and started walking. I studied the bland rocks under my feet and considered what I would do when I reached the resort. It didn't matter. I just wanted to keep walking.

I knew the owners, a retired married couple, Bing and Kellie Gibson. I recalled that they had bought the place three years earlier from the Woolerys. The Woolerys' main claim to fame, besides the resort, was that their son was Chuck Woolery, one-time host of *Love Connection*. He used to visit them and eat at the local restaurants. That was juicy stuff in a small town like Battle Lake. We didn't see a lot of stars in the North Country.

The closest I had come to someone famous was a girl in high school, Savannah, who had appeared on *Puttin' on the Hits* the summer after our sophomore year. She mouthed and wiggled to "Shout" by Tears for Fears with the help of a cousin of hers from Saint Paul. When she was in California filming her episode, she rode on the same elevator as Telly Savalas. She hadn't won on the show, but that double dose of fame had been heady to all of us. We went around saying his trademark "Who loves ya, baby?" for most of our junior year of high school.

I thought of this as I came upon the main lodge of Shangri-La, and I wondered what I would say to the Gibsons if they were around. They were a sweet couple and always went out of their way to talk to me whenever we'd cross paths, but we had never hung out socially. In fact, I had never even been as far as Shangri-La and had only seen it from the lake. Except for the beach, the whole place was heavily treed and private.

Once inside the trees, the setting was spectacular. The main lodge was as big as a church, but its stained wood siding and cedar shakes blended with the oaks and birch that shaded the grounds. The little island was perfectly tended, with an immaculate lawn right up to the beach, the whole length of it. I could see the four servants' buildings that now served as cabins for any guests who chose not to stay in the bed and breakfast that was the main lodge. The matching landscaping around all four of the buildings consisted of miniature lilacs, flowering chokecherry bushes, and shade-friendly perennials like hostas, columbine, and lupine. Judging from the piles of lake toys and fishing gear outside the cabins, the place was full. I wondered what finding a dead body near the beach was going to do to business.

I heard children giggling and spotted a group of four kids, all under ten, playing on the metal swing set on the far side of the cabin. I ducked around the front of the lodge so I wouldn't be seen. I felt like I was trespassing, but I would probably be better off acting like I belonged here. I straightened out my unconscious hunch and told myself to walk with confidence. I rubbed my hands over my face and wiggled my nose, which was turning stiff with sunburn. I belonged here. The earth was my domain.

I strode around to the front of the lodge and past the group of seven or eight people sitting on the front deck, sipping iced tea and speculating on what the boats were doing out front. I nodded at them like I was a guest, too, and went inside.

If the outside of the lodge was spectacular, the inside was Taj Mahal. The floors were a gleaming maple, rich and red, the ceilings were fifteen feet high, and the decorating was a blend of rustic and exquisite. I felt like I was in a spacious English hunting lodge.

I remembered Shirly Tolverson saying the Addamses' bedroom was upstairs, and I suddenly knew that was where I was headed. Shirly had made it pretty clear that he had caught Mrs. Krupps, the necklace-losing guest from out East, snooping there, and that she appeared to be hiding something. That caused a suspicious chain of events: she lost a diamond necklace, Shirly and the other help were fired, and the Addams sold the place. I was curious what had drawn her to the closet, if maybe there was something unusual about it, but mostly I wanted to see what the bedroom of a fabulously wealthy couple looked like. The Gibsons had taken pains to keep the rest of the lodge authentic, and I was betting that the master bedroom was fantastic. With any luck, it would be the bedroom they stayed in and therefore not a guest room with a lock on the door. I might be able to snoop around.

I walked out of the front sitting room and into the dining room. The table that ruled the dining space could seat twenty people comfortably, and there was still area to spare. The Gibsons had placed antique furniture in the corners, and the curtains floating on the light breeze looked handmade. Fresh daisies and snapdragons were scattered in vases around the room.

I heard voices behind me as I tiptoed up the stairs. I needn't have bothered walking lightly. The voices belonged to some Shangri-La guests who ignored me as they walked past the dining hall and into another wing of the first floor. I continued upward. The steps were hand carved out of expensive wood and wouldn't be caught dead creaking, so I again reminded myself I didn't need to sneak. I had decided that if I ran into the Gibsons, I would say I was there to tell them about the body I had found. It seemed like a neighborly thing to do, and it was good cover. Anyone else who noticed me would think I was a guest.

At the top of the stairs, I really got a feel for the size of the lodge. The steps wound up the middle of the building and divided the open-area landing of the second floor. If I went left or right off the stairs, I would walk in a square and be able to peer down into all the main rooms below me. Off of this square were eight doors, two on each side, and I guessed they all led to bedrooms or suites.

I walked around the first bend of the square but didn't try any of the doors because they all looked too normal to be the master bedroom of a man who would name his summer home Shangri-La. Sure enough, a second hallway led off the main square. This offshoot was lit by a string of triangular skylights, and I walked down it. *Bingo.* At the end of the hallway was a door straight out of Camelot. It had gilded leaves carved into its heavy wood, and the doorknob was a glittering crystal—it had to be the master bedroom. I felt the ball with my hand, and it was warm. Then it started to turn.

I jumped back, and all my excuses fell out of my head. Why was I in the hallway of a main lodge where I wasn't staying, about to go into a room where I didn't belong? Best to run. I turned as the main door opened, rushed my guilty hand through my hair, and hunched my shoulders over.

"... the rocks must be goddamn invisible if they're in that room, because I've—Mira?" The male voice went from exasperated to dangerously annoyed.

I kept walking.

"What're you doing here, Mira?"

I pushed my hair behind my ears and turned. It was Happy Hands, his sharp eyebrows drawn together in a V over his dark, angry eyes. "Hi, Jason." I would have been less surprised to see him at a spelling bee, but I tried to hide it. Jason and I had never really spent any one-on-one time together, even before he assaulted me. For him to appear at my house last night and in Shangri-La today was too much bad luck.

He was decked out in zebra-striped Zubaz, a white Coors Light T-shirt, and the same shoes he wore when he had accosted me the night before. Apparently he hadn't gone far after that encounter. He didn't look much happier than he had when I'd last seen him, either. I made a weak attempt at a joke. "No room at the parents', huh?"

He scowled at me, and then was pushed aside by a heavily jeweled hand. "Get out of my way, Jason! Gawd! You make a better window than a door." The hand was followed by a bleached blonde with a heavy New Jersey twang, probably in her early thirties but a heavy smoker judging by the rasp of her voice and the premature crow's feet around her green eyes. She looked at me. "Hi. You staying here?"

I smiled back at her and held out my hand. "Nope, I live up the road. You a friend of Jason's?"

She rolled her eyes in an "unfortunately" kind of way, and shook my hand. Her fingernails were claw-like and red, and I wondered if they were what had left the mark on Jason's back, either in ecstasy or pain. "The big dope." She smiled at him and rubbed his cheeks like he was a naughty child, even though he was a good seven inches taller and eighty pounds heavier than her. "I'm Samantha Krupps. Who're you?"

I felt a weird jolt of déjà vu. Krupps. The last name of the woman who had lost the diamond necklace many years earlier. "Mira. You from around here?"

She smiled, revealing poison-berry lipstick flecks on her teeth. "I'm from New York. Jason dragged me out here for a little vacation. Aren't we lucky that we found this place?"

Luck, indeed. I smelled something fishy, and it wasn't even me. "Where'd you two meet?"

"Oh, we—" Before Samantha could finish, Jason slammed the door shut behind him, locked it, grabbed her hand, and pulled her down the hall.

Before he went down the stairs, he turned to glare at me. "After you."

"I'm staying. I want to talk to the Gibsons."

He released Samantha's hand, and I could see the white marks his grip had made on her skin. He strode toward me and leaned down so he was nose to nose with me. "The Gibsons went to town. You should go home. You look like shit."

The message was clear: he wasn't leaving until I was. Now that I knew the lay of the land, I could always come back when this ape wasn't babysitting the room. No way was he getting the last word in, though. "You know, Jason, you're a big red asshole."

I tried to sail past him, my nose in the air, but he grabbed my arm and twisted it behind me. It burned like the snakebites my friends and I used to give each other in grade school, but it didn't feel like Jason was going to stop before my skin slid off under his grip. I stared haughtily at him—he wasn't going to see that I was scared and too tired to fight back. He opened his mouth to say something, but instead pushed me toward the stairs. I walked past Samantha, who was looking over the stair rail.

"Nice meeting you," I said to her, and then walked down the stairs, out the door, and up the road, acting like I was doing it of my own free will. Truth be told, I was happy to get away. I needed some time to think. Jason was looking for "rocks," and I didn't think he was after granite. He was in town with a Krupps and was clearly looking for far more than a five-thousand-dollar reward for a lost necklace. Hmm. It sure would be a good story if I found the "rocks" first, and as a bonus, I bet Jason would be upset, maybe even feel assaulted and betrayed. The race was on.

SEVEN

I WENT BACK TO the doublewide and stacked carbonated water cans in front of the inside of each door so I'd wake up if a dead body or Jason came after me. A quick look around assured me that everything was as I had left it. The rust-colored sectional couch still dominated the front living area, the kitchen was still spotless, and there wasn't anyone in my bedroom, master bath, or laundry room.

The doors to the spare bedroom and office were closed, as they always were. I had shoved most of Sunny's clutter into them when she left. I liked a lot of green and open space, and besides the book-shelves, television, and plants in the living room, there was nothing to dust. Tiger Pop and Luna followed me in and watched me as I tore open the fridge, ravenous. I pulled out some honey wheat ba-gels and organic cream cheese. While the bagel toasted, I snatched the tomato off the windowsill where it had been ripening and sliced it thin. When the bagel popped up, I smeared on the cream cheese, stacked on as many fresh tomato slices as I could, and salted and peppered the whole pile. The first bagel, I didn't taste. When I got halfway through the second one, I slowed down enough to enjoy it.

While I chewed noisily, Tiger Pop found his favorite spot on the brown afghan draped over the couch and closed his eyes in ecstasy as he kneaded the yarn and soaked up a patch of sunlight. I had named him after my second favorite candy (behind Nut Goodies, of course), a sucker almost too sweet to eat and the same colors as my kitty—patches of white splashed through orange and red. Luna watched me eat, hopeful, and I gave her the last nub of my bagel out of sympathy. She caught it midair.

Tummy full, I walked over to the fridge and pulled out a bottled water. The well water here was not drinkable, although if I'd had a glass I'd have met my mineral content for the day. The sinks were stained orange from the iron level, and the water always emitted a faint toilet smell. I brought the bottle of Aquafina into my bedroom and passed out on my clean, made bed, too tired to undress or even crawl under the blankets. I slept so hard that I dreamt I was sleeping. The sun was cooling when I finally lurched out of bed, and I felt no more rested than before I had lain down.

I forced myself into clean clothes and drove to the yellow-bricked Battle Lake Public Library. This was the only Internet connection I had, and before I did anything else, I was going online to order a Taser. Between the dead body and Jason's animosity, I was feeling a clear breach in personal security. I parked my car in the empty lot behind the building and decided to go to the Fortune Café coffee shop for some green tea to perk myself up before I went online in search of crime-prevention weapons.

The streets were pretty busy for a Sunday night, which meant two cars passed me and there was an older couple walking toward me. We were on the same block before I realized the couple was the Gibsons, my neighbors and owners of Shangri-La. They must have been eating out. I considered turning around and walking the other way, but they caught sight of me and waved me over.

Bing was a short man, maybe five-foot-five, and his head was entirely hairless except for his bushy white eyebrows, perched like an umlaut on his face. He had been a pilot in a previous life and carried himself with quiet confidence. Kellie was the tall one, pushing five-eight, and she always wore her long gray hair in a French twist. She met Bing after he had broken his leg in a skiing accident and been referred to the clinic where she was a physical therapist. Now, they both were living out their dream of owning a bed and breakfast.

"Mira! How're you doing?" Kellie held out her hand and smiled warmly at me. Bing did the same.

I suddenly felt personally responsible for the existence of a dead body in front of their resort and ducked my head. "I'm good." I wondered if they knew. According to Jason, they had been in town when I came across the corpse. I sure didn't want to be the one to tell them. "How's business?"

They looked at each other and chuckled. "Good enough to raise the dead," Kellie said, stifling a guffaw.

I recoiled. If they knew about the body, that was one heck of a tacky thing to say. "I don't know what's funny."

"Didn't you hear? A diver came across what she thought was a dead body on Whiskey Lake early this afternoon. Right out front of our beach, matter of fact. Turns out it was just a stuffed wetsuit tied to a rock and made to look like a drowned carcass."

My eyes got big and I had a genuine coughing fit. I had almost gotten myself drowned next to a fake body. Geez. That would have been as embarrassing as hitting a cow with my car, something I might also have nearly done at one time. At least the Gibsons didn't know I was the diver. I fought the urge to defend the lack of visibility underwater.

"A fake corpse? Why would anyone put a fake corpse in Whiskey Lake? Do the police know who did this?"

Kellie screwed up her face, her green eyes twinkling. "Probably some attention-getting prank related to the *Star Tribune* contest."

Boy, these two had a knack for making me feel dumb. "You guys know about the necklace contest?"

"It was actually my idea," Kellie said modestly. "I have a friend at the newspaper, and she passed the idea on to the woman who wrote the article. It's fun, don't you think?"

"Yeah, buckets of fun."

"You dive, don't you Mira? You should get a wetsuit and look for the planted necklace!" Kellie grabbed Bing's hand playfully and pulled him down the street. "We'll see you around. Why don't you come to the resort tomorrow night? The Romanov Traveling Theater troupe has agreed to give an outdoor performance, weather permitting. It's going to be a jungle magic show with jugglers and mimes and bongo players!"

That's what the doctor ordered—a night with a mime at a resort where my almost-rapist was staying, in front of which I had biffed across a fake dead body. It would be like Christmas in June. I considered taking up cigarettes again as I entered the Fortune Café. The café had been open for over seven years and was run by two local lesbians. For some odd reason, the town referred to them as "the women who played cards." It was a Lutheran euphemism for lady lovers that I didn't get. I was just glad nobody felt a need to label me based on whom I slept with. It would be "yikes" instead of "dykes."

Both Sid and Nancy wore comfortable shoes and had thin lips. Sid had short, spiky hair and preferred flannel, even in the summer, and Nancy had flowing, Crystal Gale brown hair that she pulled back with butterfly pins. Nancy's life motto was "Shit or get off the pot," and she had a plaque proclaiming this outside the bathroom door of the café. If people wanted to believe it referred to their restroom activities, that was their business.

The whole of the coffee shop smelled like cinnamon and fresh bread, and Sid and Nancy made the best decaf mochas and ginger scones this side of the Cities. The front room of the café was stocked with their personal book collection, mostly mysteries and true crime novels, and comfy furniture. I spent many a free day reading, sipping tea or coffee, and playing Scrabble with Sid when business was slow. Nancy didn't like board games.

During one of our spring word fests, I'd asked Sid why she and Nancy had come to Battle Lake. Like many a small town, this one had people with small minds who would not line up to give two proud women who happened to be gay the key to the city. Shoot, I still encountered people here who pretended they didn't hear me when I talked to them because I wasn't born in Battle Lake.

Sid spelled out QUINCE and took a drag off her coffee. "There's small minds everywhere, Mira. You can't make choices based on fear."

"I don't know. I make some of my best choices based on fear."

Sid smiled. "Nancy and I both grew up in towns the size of Battle Lake. We like the pace and the familiarity. Plus, this is the only coffee shop we found that we could afford."

"Ha! So it was money that brought you here."

"That, and the gorgeous lake and smiling faces of the locals and the great sermons Pastor Winter gives. Just give it some time, Mira, and you'll be stuck here too. In a good way. This town has a lot to offer."

I laid the D, I, and S tiles in front of the word BELIEF that she had put down four turns ago. Fifteen points, doubled because the D fell on a pink double-word-score square. I loved it when things worked out like that.

"Sid, did you know that Alfred M. Butts invented Scrabble?"

"Yeah, and I. M. Alezbo is going to win it," she said. "Pay attention!"

I smiled at this memory of Sid's humor as I walked up to her at the counter. The smell of fresh-roasted coffee beans pushed the thought of ordering green tea out my ear.

"Mira! Is it too late in the night for a decaf mocha?" she asked.

"Only if you didn't just find a fake dead body in Whiskey Lake?"

"That was you!" Sid turned and hollered for Nancy. "Nance! That dead body in Whiskey Lake, that wasn't really dead or a body? Guess who found it!"

Nancy showed up at the front counter wiping her flour-covered hands on a rainbow-colored apron that read "One Recruit Short of a Toaster Oven." She grinned broadly when she saw me, her bright smile gentling her rough features. "My money is on our resident body-finder, Ms. James herself."

"Bingo." I fished in the pockets of my cutoffs for money. "Since you guys already know about the pseudo-body, I suppose you know about the diamond necklace and the *Star Tribune* contest?"

"Old news, sweets. Tell Ron at the *Recall* to get his hands out of his wife's pants and onto a keyboard, preferably with a washing in between. Most of the town knows about the contest."

"Why am I always the last one to know?" I asked.

"You're an outsider, hon." Nancy put her arm around Sid and gave her a peck on the cheek. "It takes a while for this town to accept you."

"Pshaw. Give me some coffee. I'm off to order a Taser and maybe have a couple drinks at Clyde's to see what else everyone knows that I don't."

Sid operated the gurgling machine and added extra chocolate and whipped cream to my drink. She winked at me as she slid it across the counter. "Two-fifty. Anything else?"

"Call me if you hear something that sounds like news, 'kay? I'm supposed to be a reporter."

"I'll give you a call if I hear anything, honey." She patted my wrist.

"Thanks." I sipped gingerly at the creamy hot coffee, which felt like manna on my throat, still sore from heaving lake water, and headed out the door in search of weaponry and answers. The short evening walk to the library was pleasant. On Sunday nights, the weekend tourists packed up and returned to the Cities, leaving Battle Lake warm and relatively quiet. The chairs outside of Granny's Pantry were packed, full of sticky kids nursing triple-decker waffle cones and playing tag around their parents' legs. Otherwise, it was just my coffee and me. I took a sip and fished in my pockets for the library keys.

Lartel, the former head librarian and a guy with a freaky doll fetish, had always kept a key under the fake rock out front. He had disappeared in May shortly after Jeff was killed. He hadn't even taken the time to put his house up for sale, so there was always a possibility that he would return. When I got his job, I'd removed the key and convinced the town to change the locks.

I was now the only one who held the keys, and I kept the place pretty clean. That's why Kennie's Minnesota Nice brochure with a paper pocket full of business cards stuck to the outside of the tall and narrow library window immediately caught my attention. I shoved one of her cards in my back pocket and promised myself I'd find some way to get Kennie to infect Jason's life.

Inside the library, the smell of old paper and slick magazines was still the first thing to greet me, but since I had started running the ship, there was a whiff of sandalwood incense underneath it as well. There were also far more plants in the place, mostly ferns and succulents, my favorites. I had them crawling in the windows, and if the sun was just right, the kid's area under the south window was lit up like a jungle.

There were twelve rotating carrels near the front desk, and they housed mysteries, true crime, and romance. To the right was the children's area, and straight back were the stacks. The far wall held a pretty decent magazine selection, though I may have been the only one who read the monthly copy of *Spin*.

I marched straight to the front desk computer, booted it up, and found the article I had started on the diamond necklace. I added some angles from my interview with Shirly without giving away his reluctance to go on the record about whether or not the diamond was real or his suspicion there was something else going on at Shangri-La that summer—that was something I wanted to look into for myself before announcing it to the world. I proofread the article until I was satisfied it was error-free and not too obviously plagiarized from the *Star Tribune* original, and sent it off to Ron.

After I clicked on "Send," I ran a search on "Taser." I didn't really know what they were beyond a legal way for me to defend myself without having to go through five years of tae kwon do. Turns out they shot little electric bullets, nonlethal and nonpenetrating, which resulted in "Electro-Muscular Disruption." I gathered this was cop-speak for "You'll be so buggered by electricity that it'll be half an hour before you can slap a mosquito off your own ass."

Unfortunately, the gun-like Tasers were out of my price range, so I opted for a fifty-five-dollar Z-Force stun gun, which promised to deliver 300,000 volts to any creep who got within arm's reach. It looked like a mean black vibrator with two metal prongs at the end. I knew I'd have a hard time not testing it out, but I had a feeling fate would provide me with that opportunity soon, and I was old enough to know you should always listen to your hunches. I paid twenty-five extra bucks for same-day shipping on my order, shut down the computer, and took off for Bonnie & Clyde's.

Once on the road, I cranked my window as far open as it would go to let the frog songs and sweet green breeze wash in. Minnesota is an incredible place to live, but we natives learn at a very young age that for this privilege we must pay a tithe, usually in blood. We're first indoctrinated while we're still in diapers. A summer day spent in the shallow, still part of the lake results in a chocolate-chip-shaped leech nesting between our peas-in-a-pod toes. This leads to the wood tick that attaches itself to the front of our ear lobe when we're five. We think it's the closest we'll come to an earring for many years, so through luck and cunning we manage to hide it from our mom until it's a corpulent gray blob, its legs ridiculously small on its blood-stressed body.

Interspersed with all of this are the mosquitoes, which are there when the snow isn't, and when winter arrives, it brings with it winds so fierce that school is sometimes canceled simply because it's too cold to step outside. We learn the price of Minnesota's beauty at an early age. It's not a place for the faint of heart, and we wouldn't have it any other way.

It's a quiet understanding of these dynamics that makes every native Minnesotan welcome at Bonnie & Clyde's, one of two bars and four total businesses in Clitherall, if you count the post office as a business.

It was only a seven-minute ride from Battle Lake to Clitherall, and I went sixty the whole way. The only time I slowed was when I passed Delbert Larsen on the shoulder of Highway 210 driving his riding lawn mower to the bar. He had gotten his license revoked after his fifth DWI in May, but he wasn't letting that put a dent in his good times. I waved as I passed, and he made the classic "old man shaking his fist in the air" gesture back at me. Crabby bastard.

When I entered Clyde's, the cigarette smoke and pounding notes of Kid Rock raced for purchase in all my orifices big and small. The smoke won, but the music got my hips moving. I tried to look cool, staring back at all those who glanced at the jangling of the door opening, but I needn't have bothered. The place was empty except for Ruby, who was the bartender and owner, Jedediah Heike, and Johnny Leeson.

My heart pumped some extra blood to my cooter at the sight of Johnny, and I took a hard left to the bar instead of saying hi. I envied those women who could flirt—those easy-smiling, hair-flipping, ass-shaking sirens. I just wasn't comfortable putting myself out there like that. The best I could rustle up, when confronted by an attractive male, was an attention-deflecting sarcastic remark and a stiff smile. If my dating track record was any indication, this was exactly the mating dance of the emotionally unavailable male for whom foreplay is a card game. I needed to find a guy who could see past my social ineptitude to the magnificent me, like Jeff Wilson had done. "Hi, Ruby. Got any specials tonight?"

Ruby ignored me like she ignored all her customers. She shoved beer glasses upside down on the rotating scrubbers in the first of three sinks she used to wash barware. The second sink rinsed the soap off, and the third sink sanitized with some blue cleansing agent. Or at least it would have, if the toxicity of Clitherall's water didn't create a chemical reaction that made the blue tablet black and the water smell like old broccoli.

Two years earlier, a sales rep had come to Clyde's trying to sell a gross of cocktail napkins that patrons could splash a drop or two of their drink onto to see if it had been spiked with any date-rape drugs. That was the only time I had ever seen Ruby laugh out loud. She knew the nitrates in the town water neutralized everything but alcohol, for good or bad. It was part of the charm of the place, and besides, Clitherall was the home of the oldest married couple in the five-state area. The water couldn't be all bad.

Ruby swiped her wet hands on her jeans, tipped up one of the still-dripping beer glasses, and poured me a Lite draft. I thanked her, slid two singles onto the low spot of the bar, and watched her hands carefully. She had a way of taking my money and assuming her tip without me ever seeing it. The game was worth the 80 percent gratuity.

Ruby was in her early seventies and had owned Bonnie & Clyde's for decades. Her husband had built the place, and she'd kept it running herself after he died. The inside was a visual disharmony of wood and lights, with holes in the floor that allowed customers to watch Ruby change kegs below, and bathroom doors that didn't lock. The chairs were plastic, elementary-school style, and the tables were mismatched, some of them handmade and some of them folding card tables. This comfortable rot was contrasted with a sparkly, modern jukebox, pristine pool tables, and a buttery, elegant main bar.

I was considering how long I should let the beer sit in my glass before the alcohol killed the nitrates, or vice versa, when there was a tap on my shoulder.

"Mira, hey, cool. Why don't you come hang out with me and Johnny?"

I smiled at Jed, thinking I'd like to hang *off* of Johnny for a while. For a minute, I was worried that Johnny must be a pothead if he hung around with Jed, but then I remembered I hung out with Jed sometimes, too. I think the three of us didn't bump into one another more often because Johnny spent most nights playing in a local band and giving piano lessons to old ladies and young girls. He was a Battle Lake native, and he had left for college in Wisconsin to study plant biology about five years earlier. I don't know if he finished his degree or not, but I did know he returned to his hometown the summer before under less-than-happy circumstances. My local friend Gina said he got kicked out of college for knifing a guy or stealing rare plants from the college greenhouse, she wasn't sure which. I refused to believe either.

I leaned over to check out the man for all seasons over by the pool table, admiring the thick ropes in his neck and arm as he tipped his head back to finish his beer. Johnny was bright and healthy and open. Clearly, he was not my type. With the exception of my short tryst with Jeff, I went for the dark brooders, the guys who disguised vapidity as introspection.

I even went out with one attractive slacker because he liked dark chocolate and I wanted to believe that was proof of his intelligence. I could no longer buy that illusion after he let me read his poetry. It all rhymed, and every poem was about the band Van Halen. The only one that I can remember specifically was titled "David Lee Roth, Thou Art the Flame to My Moth."

No, Johnny would definitely stand out in the short lineup of my past loves, but I couldn't deny his earthy appeal. I wanted to get down and dirty with him, literally. I decided to take this bull by the horns as I followed Jed back to the table. Seeing Johnny twice in one day without having to stalk him must be a sign. I could be cool. Right?

"Hey, Jay, you see Mira was here?" Jed said.

I held out my hand and smiled into Johnny's eyes. "Twice in one day. It must be fate."

At least, that's what I swear to God I meant to say. Unfortunately, it came out as, "Twice in one day. This lust can't wait."

I honestly shouldn't be let out of the house some days. Thank God I'm a mumbler when I'm nervous. It's nature's way of balancing out the fact that dorky stuff rushes out of my mouth like vomit when I'm feeling awkward.

Johnny held on to my hand and leaned his ear close to my mouth. "What?"

I breathed the clean spice of his thick, sun-lightened hair, and lightning bolts shot out of my crotch. If smoke started rising from my nether region, I would never be able to look him in the eye again.

"I just said it's nice to see you again. You know, here at Bonnie & Clyde's, where before it was at the Last Resort." Hmm. That put me one sentence past cool.

He nodded. "Yah. Say, I enjoyed that article on Jeff Wilson."

Jesus. He gardened, smoldered, *and* read. I was way out of my league.

"And I plant your stuff in my garden." I followed this with a twinkly guffaw and filled my mouth with beer before I said something else stupid.

For his part, Johnny smiled brilliantly and turned back to the pool game. When he was out of earshot, I turned to Jed. "Why am I such a dork?"

"Dorks rule, man. Wanna get high?"

"No thanks, Jed. How're you doing tonight?"

"Except for a little too much time with the Man, I'm good. Shit, I thought they were coming for me."

I pulled my attention from Johnny, who was leaning provocatively into the pool table as he lined up the purple four ball with the corner pocket. "The cops?"

"The cop," Jed corrected me, running his hand nervously through his curly hair. I noticed he was wearing a black Pink Floyd T-shirt with a rainbow prism etched on the front. "Chief Gary Wohnt came by the Last Resort, dude, and his cherries were on. I had my stash flushed before he got to the main office. Good thing I only had a dime bag."

"He came to bust you?"

"Naw, and that's the kicker!" Jed slapped his knee. "He wanted a list of who we rented dive gear to. That fake body they found in Whiskey? It was wearing a Last Resort wetsuit. We stamp the name on every one of 'em. Right on the butt."

I wanted to laugh with Jed, but every time someone talked about that body, I fumed. I felt like it was a big joke at my expense, and somebody needed to pay. "So who *did* you provide gear for?"

"Aw, some tourists staying at Shangri-La, a couple staying at the Last Resort, and you."

"No one you recognized?"

"No one except Jason Blunt. You know him, don't you? I think he used to date Sunny back in the day. Boy, could that dude put away a bong. He had a mean streak like a mule if you crossed him, though."

My heart made its way out of my chest and lumped in my throat. "Jason rented a dive suit from you?"

"Three dive suits, three BCs, three of everything, the day before you got yours. Why? You think he planted the body?"

I suddenly felt very tired. My cocky spell had passed, and I had had enough Jason Blunt for one day. "That's totally possible, Jed." The question was, why? It must be connected to the jewels he was after. I had to find out more.

I brought my unfinished beer up to the counter and saw that my two dollars had disappeared even though Ruby had been at the far end of the bar the entire time I'd been talking to Johnny and Jed. I said a quick goodbye to both, and thought for a moment that

Johnny's eyes lingered on my mouth as he smiled at me. No, must have been the lighting. Anyhow, I was too concerned about Jason's current mischief to have more than a parting lustful thought about Johnny Leeson.

EIGHT

I SLEPT FITFULLY THAT night and woke at least four times, wishing I had my stun gun under my pillow. On the fifth wake-up, I seriously considered moving myself to a corner of the spare room under all of Sunny's stored junk. An intruder would not look for me there, and I could catch some hidden z's. I quickly discarded that idea, though, refusing to be scared in my own bed in my own home.

At four a.m., I gave up on wrestling with the sandman and took my knotty head outside. The air was hot on cool, the leftovers of a ninety-degree day losing out to the quiet morning chill. I could feel the repercussions of the previous day's heat in the tightness of my sunburned nose and shoulders as I stretched. Outside, the animals didn't know whether to make night or morning sounds, and my presence threw another wrench into their song. I sat on the front deck, closing my eyes so I could better hear the rustlings in the woods and smell the mystery of Whiskey Lake and an early summer morning.

I soon realized I wasn't comfortable sitting, either. I had too much nervous energy. I got off my butt, the sweat shorts I had thrown on wet from the dew, and walked past the barn down to my vegetable garden near the lake. I had tilled this area in April, and though I still had to fight the pigweed and thistle for ownership, it was turning out to be a good location with a full day of sun.

The marigolds I had recently planted were the tallest growths in the garden. I could smell their acridness even with their orange and yellow heads closed to the bright moon. I traditionally planted a thick square of marigolds and catnip first thing around all my vegetable gardens. With their natural insecticide properties, they were soldiers guarding the hairy innocence of my zucchini, carrot, bean, pea, and corn sprouts.

This year I had also planted dill, for two reasons. First, Johnny had told me it would repel aphids as well as the spider mites attracted by my marigolds and would draw the tomato worms away from my heirloom Red Brandywines. Second, although I had a pretty green thumb, I could not grow cucumbers to save my soul. Try as I might in many different soils with many different varieties, from Tendergreen Burpless to White Spineless, I couldn't get the seedlings to grow much past germination. I figured the dill would serve as an enticement, like, "If you grow, I'll let you be a pickle." Pickling was the Valhalla of the vegetable world.

It was my mom who had turned me on to gardening. Every summer, she tilled up a huge section of open land between the outbuildings on the hobby farm and planted every vegetable that would grow in west central Minnesota—and some, like garlic and sweet potatoes, that wouldn't. She was a gifted and optimistic gardener, and although I hated planting and weeding when I was younger, I loved to watch her face when she worked. All the lines left her forehead and around her mouth, and although she never looked happy, she looked peaceful, like she was in the right place at the right time. I only saw her look like that when she was in her garden.

I stepped through the opening I had left in my bug-fighting border and mucked over to the far side of the garden. The black dirt was speckled with dew and still warm from the sun rays of the day before. My toes squished through the top layer of light dew-mud and into the looser earth below. I kneeled at my row of carrots, one knee on each side. The shaggy sprouts were thick; I didn't have enough patience to plant the microscopic seeds carefully or the heart to thin them after they sprouted, so I treated carrots as an ornamental crop.

The moon was full enough for me to distinguish carrot from weed, and I quickly got my patter down, popping the thistle and leafy spurge easily from the moist ground. As I worked, my knees sank into the dirt and my mind focused. Jason was back in town, and he had brought with him Samantha Krupps, a bleached blonde with a Jersey accent who was likely related to the woman who "lost" the necklace in Whiskey Lake decades ago.

I was sure there was more to the original Krupps story than simply a lost necklace, and overhearing Jason in the master bedroom at Shangri-La had confirmed my hunch that there was something hidden in that room. Maybe it was the missing necklace, along with the rest of the jewels that had gone missing that summer eighty and some odd years ago.

I was sure if I got in the bedroom I could find the jewels. This feeling was probably tied to my childhood as a stasher. Back then, hiding my valuables had given me a feeling of control over my life. I hid flattened money in the cracks in my window sash, sea glass in the knothole in my closet, and my diary under my bedsprings.

My favorite hoard was a cache of glittering rhinestones that I had started collecting at garage sales when I was six. I would save up my allowance to scour the old jewelry piled on the front card table of every rummage sale. After many years, I had acquired quite a collection, and it was still hidden in the floorboards of my old bedroom. I wanted something to return home to, something that consistently made me happy, and I wondered if Mrs. Krupps had had the same urge all those years ago.

I just didn't know how the *Star Tribune* article tied into the return of Jason and appearance of Samantha Krupps. Was it coincidence that the newspaper article ran at the same general time they'd arrived looking for lost jewels, or was there a bigger plan unfolding here, one beyond my vision?

And what would Jason and Samantha have to gain by outfitting and planting a fake dead body in Whiskey Lake? If they hoped to scare off people looking for the contest's necklace early, their time would have been better spent searching for the real necklace themselves, since they obviously knew about the real diamond long before the rest of the world. This made me wonder whether the Gibsons were in on all this. Kellie said she had tipped the newspaper to the whole necklace story. Clearly, I would have to do some investigative reporting at the Romanov show at Shangri-La that evening, despite my misgivings about crowds and theater types. And I needed to sneak into the master bedroom to find out what was going on.

I was weeding the peas by now. The vines were so extensive I had to flip them side to side like long green hair over dirt shoulders to reach the weeds underneath. I would have kept weeding, ignoring the pinks of the rising sun, if the melancholy cry of a loon on the lake hadn't pulled me out of my thoughts. I sat back on my heels and looked for the bird, but the shadows played tricks on my eyes. I brushed off my knees and went inside.

After a long, refreshing shower, I slapped on some ChapStick, made a yogurt, frozen berry, and banana smoothie, and headed to town to get the *Recall* and open up the library.

My article was on the front page. I had titled it "Find One Diamond Today" because it sort of rhymed in the middle, and I hoped the "Today" made it sound fresh:

> A day in paradise could end up being a week in Shangri-La for the lucky finder of the fake diamond planted in Whiskey Lake. The *Star Tribune*, tipped off to a local legend, has placed a weighted box containing a paste diamond into Whiskey Lake, south of town on Highway 78. People may begin diving for it today, and whoever finds it first will receive $5,000 and a paid week at Shangri-La, the Whiskey Lake–based resort owned by Kellie and Bing Gibson.
>
> "[The contest] was actually my idea," Kellie Gibson said modestly. "I have a friend at the newspaper, and she passed the idea on to the woman who wrote the article."
>
> Gibson's idea had such appeal because of the deep history of the area. According to Shirly Tolverson, local historian, Randolph Addams built Shangri-La in the 1920s to be his summer home. When it was complete, he had a beautiful main lodge (what Addams called his "little cabin") and four cabins for the help, all nestled on the six-acre peninsula jutting into Whiskey Lake. During the summer of 1929, a Ms. Krupps from New York was a guest at the Addamses' lodge. While swimming, she lost her necklace, an enormous dewdrop diamond hung on a gold chain.
>
> According to Tolverson, who was working at Shangri-La the summer the necklace disappeared, "I saw her go into the water with a diamond the size of a caramel around her neck. I saw her walk out of the water without it." The guests and staff, including Tolverson, searched frantically. The diamond was never found,

and local legend has it that it is still in the lake, waiting to be discovered.

The *Star Tribune* contest, designed to bring attention to Battle Lake's beautiful topography and tourist appeal, is about finding a fake diamond, but who knows? Maybe some lucky diver will find the real thing.

I folded the paper, not entirely happy with my article because I knew there was some big picture I was missing. All I could do now, though, was wait for the morning crowd to arrive for Monday Madness. That's what I called the children's reading hour I hosted every Monday morning at ten. I thought it was a funny name, what with all the kids screaming and picking and scratching at themselves as I tried to imitate perkiness while reading *The Paper Bag Princess*.

This was my one shot to infiltrate their young minds, though, and I enjoyed it. The kids liked books for all the right reasons, and they were mostly cute, even if they had the attention span of hair on fire. The only thing I dreaded about Monday Madness was dealing with Leylanda Wilson, who brought her seven-year-old daughter, Peyton, to every reading. Peyton was put upon by the constant demands of the non-princess existence she was forced to live, which was cute on a little girl. Unfortunately, her mother had the same attitude. She always complained that I only chose books about independent girls (she was right) who usually defied society's rules (right again) and that I didn't give enough time to the "classics" like *Snow White* and *Cinderella*. This Monday, she walked in dressed in an immaculate and stiff dress suit, carrying her purse as if she had her spare heart in it, Peyton dragging behind her.

"Peyton, we will stay for one half of an hour if Ms. James is reading good stories. If not, I will read you one story of your choosing no longer than seven minutes in length, and then we will go to

Meadow Farm Foods to buy some free-range chicken and delicious whole grains."

Peyton rolled her eyes at me, and I nodded and rolled mine back. Leylanda was the most horrible kind of creature—a right-wing traditionalist who disguised herself as a granola to deflect personal criticism from her ravaging narrow-mindedness. She even wore Birkenstocks with her pressed Tommy Hilfiger jeans and polos.

"Hey, Leylanda, today I'm going to read a book about a little boy and a princess who fall in love and get married."

Leylanda eyed me suspiciously from behind her trendy, dark-rimmed glasses. "What's it called?"

"*Prince Cinders*. I think Peyton'll like it." I grabbed Peyton's hand and pulled her to the front of the yammering crowd of kids before her mom could object. The story was one of my favorites, about a prince with three cheesy brothers who think they're studs. Prince Cinders gets dumped on until his fairy godmother grants his wish to be big and hairy like his brothers. She turns him into an ape. After he turns back into himself, he and the princess fall for each other, and they live happily ever after in the castle.

I read a couple more keepers and then sent the kids back to their parents, who were scattered around the library reading paperbacks and magazines. Back at the front desk, I sorted through the books that had been returned. A lot of people were streaming through already, which was unusual for ten-thirty on a Monday. I counted heads and wondered how many were here because of the diamond necklace contest. That's when Kennie walked in.

"Hey shug doll, what's up?"

Kennie was dressed and shaped like the sun. She wore acid-yellow jelly shoes, yellow-striped pedal pushers, a plastic yellow belt with a brass buckle, and a yellow tank top made of some water-, flame-, and possibly bulletproof material. Her canary-colored sunglasses were perched on her head, but they weren't bright enough to distract from her lemon-shaded earrings that looked to be taken straight out of a blind man's tackle box. All this splendor was arranged around a camel toe the size of Egypt. And just like that, I had an idea.

"Not much, Kennie. Say, you still doing that Minnesota Nice business?"

She scrabbled over to me like I was the last krumkake at a church bake sale. "Why, yes I am, honey! In fact, I'm here now to drop off some flyers. Do y'all know someone who needs the hard truth?"

I smiled so broadly that the corners of my mouth got my eyes wet. "Sort of. It's more about justice than honesty. You free tonight?"

"Hmm. Let me see." From her yellow plastic tote bag, she pulled out a cardboard folder with a picture of two adorable kittens on the front, one sleeping on a branch and the other one clinging to the wood by one slipping claw. Underneath the photo were the words "Only the Strong Survive."

"Y'all are in luck, because Monday nights are pretty open for me. What did you have in mind?" Kennie leaned forward on the counter, squishing her boobs together over a Grand Canyon of cleavage. I caught a solid waft of her signature scent: yeasty gardenias.

I considered lying, but I didn't want to deprive her of the information she'd need to see this thing through. So I half-lied. "There's this guy in town, Jason Blunt. He used to be my boyfriend, long, long time ago, and I was really into him. In fact, I think he might have been The One."

Kennie hid her doubt with the professionalism of a free-clinic gynecologist. "Go on."

"Well, I caught him cheating on me. Like I said, he's back in town, and I—"

"And y'all want me to make his life hell tonight?"

"Yep, uh-huh. I know it's a little bit outside the purview of your Minnesota Nice business, but I thought you could maybe turn on the Kennie charm and show him a good time."

"And then dump him cold, like he dumped you?"

"Sure." I was actually thinking a night fending off Kennie's advances would be its own dose of strap oil, but whatever she needed to play this scene was fine by me. She'd buy me some time to snoop, and he'd have an evening of tuna-scented hell. "He's got a girlfriend with him, so you'll need to sidestep her."

Kennie nodded sagely, making her gargantuan earrings jingle. "Where can I find him?"

So this is what it felt like to be completely satisfied. Meow. "He's staying at Shangri-La, and I'm pretty sure he'll be at the Romanov Traveling Theater performance tonight."

"He won't know what hit him, honey."

I was banking on it.

NINE

On the way home from my long day at the library, I stopped at the Turtle Stew for some broasted chicken and jo-jos to go. The Stew was my favorite restaurant in town, because they made a mean tater-tot hotdish and had authentic Naugahyde booths. It was a great place to people-watch, too, if one was Sinclair Lewis.

When I was ordering my food, it occurred to me that I missed my friend Gina. I ordered double of everything and took it to her house.

I'd met Gina through Sunny over a decade earlier, at the annual Chief Wenonga Days street dance. Gina and Sunny had gone to high school together in Battle Lake and had both gone on to work at the Otter Tail County nursing home, one of the few jobs besides waitressing that a local girl without a college education could get by on. The two of them were tied together due to a shared history, but I loved Gina for her simple, honest company.

She was in her late twenties, built like a blonde fire hydrant, and married to her grade-school sweetheart, Leif Hokum. When

I'd met him, I'd joked that it would be nice if all potential mates came clearly labeled like that. When I realized the last name of my job-free boyfriend at the time was Kidd, I wondered if maybe they do all come plainly labeled, and no woman had ever picked up on it. Maybe it was God's way of apologizing for poor placement of the clitoris.

Gina was wearing her scrubs when I got to her one-story house in town. She had worked at the nursing home for longer than I had known her. She started as a dietary aide in high school and became a certified nursing assistant shortly after that. Last summer she had graduated from Fergus Falls Community College's nursing program with an RN degree.

She now worked four twelve-hour shifts a week, with alternating weekends. She was so tired all the time that I hardly ever saw her. She seemed exhausted but grateful when she opened her door to me.

"Hey, chickie. Where's Leif?"

She dug into the bag of broasted chicken. "Probably fishing."

Gina's husband was the typical Otter Tail County man. He was tall, dirty blonde, and sporting a burgeoning beer belly. When he wasn't hunting with his bow and arrow, gun, or crossbow, he was ice fishing, river fishing, lake fishing, or spear fishing. All this self-reliance would be awesome if a person found himself suddenly transplanted to *Little House on the Prairie*–era Minnesota, but it sure took a bite out of relationships.

"Don't you get sick of him being gone all the time?"

She shrugged and leaned back on the couch, rearranging the walleye-shaped pillows so she could get comfortable. "He's there when I need him. Besides, we just had a great talk the other night where we both agreed we need to communicate and have more fun together."

"What're you gonna do about it?"

"Drink more." She ripped a chunk of breast meat off the bone. "Shit, this was the longest day at work ever! We had two clients sneak out, four new clients move in, and a surprise visit from the state. I feel like all I do is go to work, come home, eat, watch some TV, and go to bed. And they pay me just enough to get up the next day and do it all over again. You gonna eat all those jo-jos?"

I passed her the greasy wax bag and took a pull on my Diet Dr. Pepper. "You do look tired."

"No shit. That's why nobody around here is winning any think-offs. By the end of the day, all I want to do is watch the Mary-Kate and Ashley show and go to bed." Her eyes focused on me, and her voice changed from complaining to curious. "Say, I hear Jason Blunt is staying at Shangri-La."

I knew Gina would get to the heart of my problems pretty quickly. She always did. "How'd you hear about that?"

"Linda Gundersen, friends with Jason's mom, Harriet, stopped to visit her Aunt Flo. Linda said Harriet Blunt was in a snit because Jason's girlfriend was too good to stay at their doublewide."

I snorted. "Shoot. Trailers were made for people like those two. Yeah, he's in town. He visited me in my bedroom the night before last. Thought I was Sunny."

Gina nodded knowingly. "Horn call."

"Yup. So I don't know how good of a girlfriend this chick is if he's already sleeping around."

"That don't mean anything with Blunt. He could be married to Tyra Banks and he'd still stick his bad boy in a tree if he thought he wouldn't get caught."

I shuddered at the reminder of his aggression. I filled her in on my interview with Shirly and the questions it raised and my subsequent diving expedition. I didn't mention overhearing Jason talk about the jewels he was after, because I didn't want any rumors starting before I found out more. I told her my plan for checking out the master bedroom at Shangri-La tonight.

This made me think of Kennie in her full splendor, making a little love magic for Jason.

"What're you smiling at?" Gina smiled back, her green eyes crinkling at the corners. She had a circle of grease around her mouth that she swiped at with a napkin.

"Nothing. I gotta go, anyhow. The Shangri-La show starts in a little bit." I waved my hand at the leftover chicken. "Give Leif the rest of the food. It'd be good for him to see that you can *buy* meat, too."

I was halfway to my car before I had a thought. I returned to the house and poked my head in to see Gina sucking the marrow out of a leg bone. "Hey, queen of the jungle, I don't suppose there is an off chance that Jason's mom Harriet's friend Linda Gundersen mentioned where Jason's haughty girlfriend is from?"

"Niagara County. I remember because I didn't know it was a county. I wonder if Niagara Falls is in Niagara County."

"You'd think. Mind if I use your computer for a minute?"

"Nope. Just ignore the screen saver."

Said screen saver was a picture of two deer watching a man and a woman graphically humping away on the forest floor, with the words "Look at those animals!" scrolling across the bottom. I dialed up the Internet and got online. If I knew more about Samantha, I would have more ammunition in my search.

Fortunately, we all leave a paper trail, and these days, most of us leave a cyber trail. It took me about forty-five minutes to locate and then search the online archives of Niagara County's newspapers—the *Gazette*, *Sun*, and *Democrat*—until I found what I was looking for.

There was no photo accompanying the three-week-old obituary in the *Niagara Gazette*, and the information was short and sweet: "Regina Krupps, age 104, died of heart failure in her home in Niagara Falls. Her husband, noted entrepreneur Wilson Krupps, preceded Mrs. Krupps in death. Mr. and Mrs. Krupps, along with their dear friends the Andrew Carnegie family, created the Niagara County Center for the Arts in 1940. She was attended at her death by her nurse of four years and survived by her beloved bichon frisé, Berry Blossom."

Bingo. I'll *bet* her nurse attended her, and I had a hairy feeling that nurse was in town, rooming with Jason Blunt at Shangri-La, and that her name was not really Samantha Krupps. It was just too much of a coincidence that she and Jason would arrive in town all the way from Niagara County, New York, for a vacation at the same time everyone and his dog was looking for a lost diamond necklace owned by Regina Krupps. The elderly Mrs. Krupps had spilled some beans to her nurse, who was now in town searching for a pile of rocks. Apparently, though, Mrs. Krupps had been none too specific about their location, which bought me some time.

I printed out a copy of the obituary and walked out to find Gina snoring on the couch, the corners of her mouth still greasy from the food. I pulled her shoes off, covered her with an afghan, and was out the door.

I took the gravel back roads all the way to my house, and the sweet, dusty smell of a dirt road in June filled my car. I was in a good mood, and this only increased when I saw the package waiting on my front steps. Inside was my Z-Force, battery included. It looked a little smaller than in the picture, but it wasn't the first time I had been disappointed by size, and I recovered quickly. The stun gun was black and fierce in my hand, and it had a good weight, like a heavy flashlight. I hooked up the nine-volt and practiced a menacing posture, zapping invisible rednecks.

My doorstep activity riled the birds, who flew from the treetops squawking, and I forced myself to calm down so I didn't anger the Fowl Ones. I needed all the luck I could get tonight. For good measure, I filled the bird feeders with sweet thistle and sunflower seeds and even nailed up a couple oranges for the orioles. I refrained from apologizing out loud at the bird disquiet I had incited, but just barely.

There were already quite a few cars going down the driveway I shared with Shangri-La, and after a while, people began to walk down the mile and a half of road because there was no room to park on the island. When I counted more than forty people heading down there, I blended in with the crowd. I rarely carried a purse, but tonight I had dug out a hobo-sized one from the back of my closet to hide the reassuring weight of my freshly charged zapper and to stow away any long-lost jewelry I might chance across. I took advantage of the extra room in the purse to carry along a flashlight, a skeleton key that I had scored at a rummage sale, and some gum.

As I approached the resort grounds, the sun was setting on the west side of Whiskey. The light was spectacular, slicing through trees and across people to create backlit shadows. The general feel of the crowd was light, and there was joking and laughter. I heard talk of fireworks later, but much of the conversation centered on the fake body found in the lake. I fell in with a small group of people, all in their late forties or early fifties, and all of them dressed like out-of-town golfers.

The short, broad man I was directly behind spoke. "Gawd, I'd hate to be the idiot who found that stuffed dive suit. I heard whoever it was was pretty scared."

My fingers itched to grab the zapper. Damn tourists, judging me. I bet I could bump up against this guy and drop him without taking my hand out of my purse. I walked closer to the man talking, and I kept my eyes pasted on his comb-over.

"Doesn't take Einstein to tell a human body from a stuffed wetsuit!"

The man and his friends laughed. Two more feet and I'd be at his backside. I wondered how much of a buffer his back fat would provide him as I cradled the black plastic zapper in the security of my purse. In the dark of my hobo bag, the stun gun felt like at least seven inches.

"Let's hope the ditz doesn't have a driver's license! Probably can't tell a stop sign from a tree."

One more step. I would zap and blend back in the crowd. It'd be a pleasant way to begin tonight's festivities.

"I hope she buys a flashlight so she can find her ass to shit."

Half a step. I hit the on button and heard a soft crackle of electricity. I leaned in, hypnotized by the rhythm of his large rear cheeks rolling one over the other like ships on the storm of his thighs.

Crack! The loud boom shocked me, and I dropped the stun gun in my purse, my hand falling off the button. Weak lights burned the sky, competing with the setting sun for attention, and sparkled down to earth like crashing fireflies. I smelled the sulfur and prepared myself for another round of fireworks in the twilight sky. The crowd around me stopped and oohed.

I walked past the group I had been tailing, glaring at the guy who had been knocking me. He smiled appreciatively at my ass and turned his attention back to the sky. I continued on to the mayhem of Shangri-La Island.

Children were screaming and chasing one another as a last firework shot out from the public access and over the island. Apparently, they were just meant to announce the party. All around me, people were mingling and smiling, drinks in their hands as they rode the excitement of outdoor entertainment on a warm summer evening. The theater troupe was providing preshow distractions in the only clearing on the island. A juggler danced around the tiki torches lighting the natural stage, a unicycling clown pedaled back and forth to the delighted glee of the kids watching, and a man in a tuxedo tossed candy from stilt level. Two small figures dressed as Tweedledum and Tweedledee rolled around on the ground, and I couldn't tell from my spot if they were tiny adults or children.

There was a tropical theme blended in with the Renaissance feel of the Romanov entertainment, probably created in honor of the "island" of Shangri-La. Bongo players dressed in grass skirts and leis pounded a tribal beat on the periphery of the cleared spot, and island dancers swayed around them. The entertainment's mingling of the tropics with Shakespeare was unsettling, like interspecies mating, and I wondered how much this spectacle cost and how the Gibsons were paying for it. There was no cover charge, and only a handful of people here were paying guests. For the second time in as many days, I considered the possibility that the Gibsons were on the black end of this whole diamond deal.

I sidled closer to the main stage and looked around for familiar faces. I thought I spotted Jed playing one of the bongos, but the flickering light of the tiki torches made it hard to make out details.

"You need to stay close to your mother, and don't eat anything fried or with sugar."

I turned and saw Peyton and Leylanda standing five feet behind me. Peyton was executing a little-girl hip wiggle to the tropical beat, and Leylanda was grasping her hand tightly.

"Hey, Peyton!" I danced my way over to the little girl and we both boogied for a minute, much to the chagrin of Leylanda. "This looks like fun, eh?"

Leylanda stared icily at me. "Peyton, this is not *fun*. This is culture, and we are here to see a theater performance. Say goodbye to Ms. James."

I put out my hand, and Peyton shook it, deftly palming the Fruit Stripe gum I had concealed there. "See ya around, Peyton."

"See ya."

I walked away from the center of activity and around to the front of the lodge. Samantha Krupps was sitting on the front steps smoking a cigarette stuck in one of those long black-and-white holders that Natasha used on *Rocky and Bullwinkle*. I glanced around for Jason but didn't see him, so I walked over to her.

"Hello, Samantha."

When she turned to look at me, I could see her black eye, sullen and purplish under her unnaturally dark eyebrows.

"Wow, that's a shiner."

"No shit."

All of her chattiness from the day before was gone, and I saw no reason to play at small talk. "Jason hit you?"

She dragged deep off her cigarette. Her eyes looked hazel in the gathering night, and I could see the black roots at her hairline. She scowled into the distance.

"What city did you say you're from?"

"I didn't."

"Niagara County, I think you said."

She looked at me from the corners of her eyes and tensed up. I knew she wanted to look around for Jason, but she showed admirable restraint.

"So, you any relation to the woman who lost the diamond necklace here in the late twenties, Samantha?"

"People call me Sam."

She was talking. I needed to keep her going as long as possible, because I knew as soon as Jason showed up, she'd shut down. "Hi, Sam." I smiled at her and hoped it was open and friendly. "What's there to do in Niagara County?"

"Not much, unless you like catering to tourists." She smiled without humor. "Must be like being here, almost. I was a CNA for a while, a waitress here and there, sold garbage at gift shops. You name it, I did it."

I knew from Gina that a CNA was a certified nursing assistant, and with the proper training, a CNA could be a home health aide. I decided to bluff. "I know who you took care of when you were nursing."

"You mean my aunt? So?"

Her self-assurance caught me off guard. I was certain Regina Krupps didn't have any living relatives, or they would have been mentioned in her obituary. "So, I know she was the one who lost the diamond necklace in this lake. Regina Krupps."

Sam looked genuinely bored and pressed her thumb and forefinger together softly and slowly, like she was applauding the tiniest show.

I changed tacks, determined to regain the upper hand. "How'd you meet Jason?"

Sam took a final puff on her cigarette and ground it into the side of the stairs. She started to insert another one in her holder, and then tossed her holder into the bushes and slapped the cigarette straight in her mouth. "He came to a shop I was working at part-time. He wanted to get married to this fat redhead. We sold wedding packages, sort of like Vegas. He took one look at me and left her." She laughed icily. "Aren't I lucky?"

I ignored the question. "Why'd you come out here?"

"To meet Jason's family." She fidgeted, dodging the question and avoiding my eyes.

"So you and Jason do any diving since you got here?"

"Ha! You couldn't get me to go in a lake to save a baby. If I can't see the bottom, I don't get wet."

This jolted me. I assumed Jason had rented three sets of gear so he and Sam would each have a set, with one set left over for the fake body. If she didn't dive, Jason had an unseen accomplice who was probably a lot scarier than Sam.

A cold hand grabbed my neck, and I squealed. I turned to face the vacant smile of the ringmaster, who, dressed as a lion tamer, had given me the Romanov flyer in the nursing-home lobby yesterday. "We need a lovely lady to help us get this show started!"

He yanked me toward the makeshift stage, and I stopped struggling when I realized all eyes were on us and the music had stopped. Talk about not blending into a crowd. I could be naked and in flames and be less obvious.

"Ladies and gentlemen! Welcome to the world-renowned Romanov Traveling Theater!" His voice carried across the island and over the lake. The bongo players sprinkled throughout the crowd started slapping their skins in a slow and steady rhythm while chanting a low "Hiya, ha hiya."

"Tonight, we have a rare treat for you! In addition to the enticing entertainment provided by our island performers, you will get a preview of the local production of William C. Shakespeare's *The Taming of the Shrew*!"

William C.? Hadn't it been William S. before? Who were these Romanovs? It was now full dark outside the circle of tiki-torch light, and I tried to slink away into the inkiness. The ringmaster snatched me back.

"This beatific lady has agreed to take part in our opening extravaganza by partaking in our disappearing act! Lady, have we met before?"

I nodded my head yes.

"The lady says no! This is our first meeting! Island assistants, please bring out the magic case."

There was a somber bongo roll, and two of the skirt-clad bongo players hoisted a heavy box to the center of the earthen stage. The box was about five and a half feet tall, and from a distance, I'm sure it looked ornate. Up close, I could see it was covered in cheap plastic designed to look like carved wood. There was a door on the front without a doorknob. The ringmaster tapped the door, stepped inside and then out to show that it was a real box, and pounded the three sides to show it was solid.

"Assistants, please lead our lovely volunteer inside!"

I was starting to panic. Public speaking is bad, but public disappearing is worse. The bongo players grabbed my wrists and dragged me toward the box as I dug my heels in. I couldn't reach my stun gun and felt like a character in a Shirley Jackson story as the crowd hooted and hollered in glee. I turned to beg the bongo players to let me go and saw Jed grinning dopily at me.

"Jed!" I hissed. "What are you doing in a skirt and why the *hell* don't you let me go!"

"Easy money, Mira, and don't worry." His grin struck me as dopier than usual. "This is a cool trick. I got to do it once in rehearsal today. You'll be fine, dude. Just play along."

I relaxed not at all but gave up fighting as they shoved me into the box. The front closed like a coffin door, and the ringmaster's voice became muffled. I had to crouch down, my knees and shoulders scraping the cheap wood. The inside of the box smelled like sweat and vinegar.

"I will say the magic words, tap three times on the box, and show you our lovely volunteer has disappeared! Abracov, dabrocov, Romanov!"

There were three taps on the box, but I'm sure I was the only one who heard them over the deafening cracks of a fresh round of fireworks. Without warning, I was jerked out the back of the box as shards of light exploded from the front. Four hands shoved me into a container just big enough to hold me in the fetal position, and I felt myself being carried off. There was enough room to breathe but not enough to struggle. Fortunately, my hand had been clutching my purse when I was thrust into this tiny jail, and I concentrated on working it inside.

I was sweating with the exertion of small movements by the time my fingertips brushed against the solid plastic of my little soldier. I grabbed onto it, determined to force some involuntary bodily functions out of whoever was transporting me as soon as they let me out. *If* they let me out. Clearly, reappearing wasn't an integral part of this disappearing act.

I heard the sounds of the island party fade, gradually replaced by the sounds of feet on gravel. I considered yelling, but I wouldn't be heard over the noise of the party. I knew there was only one exit off Shangri-La—the strip of gravel that was the driveway—which meant there was now water on either side of me. I didn't want to give anyone a reason to dump me in it. Maybe this was just a harmless magic trick and I'd be let go as soon as I was totally out of sight of the audience. I concentrated on taking slow, deep breaths and was comforted by the familiar smell of Whiskey Lake and the plants that grew around my house.

The reverberations of road were replaced by the rustling of brush, and I knew we were in the woods about half a mile north of the Shangri-La main lodge. When you're leaving an isthmus, there's only one direction you can go, and if we weren't on the road, we were in the woods. Someone had an interest in stealing me away from tonight's action, but this seemed a pretty dramatic way to go.

Suddenly, the jostling stopped, and I was set down gently. The front of the container was opened.

"Du—"

I leaped and zapped, once on the hand held out to help me up and once on the upper shoulder of the other carrier. I looked wildly from Jed's falling face to the slumped body of the other bongo player. I recognized him from the bait shop. He had sold me a newspaper and Lemonheads last week and asked me how I liked the weather. I forced myself to blink and breathe. I knew from the footfalls I had been listening to that it was just the three of us in the woods, and two of us were currently ass-to-stars on the forest floor. I looked around and took in the two elm trees in front of me knotted together like lovers, the faint hum of the crowd on Shangri-La, and the whisper of breeze in the treetops. I was stiff from my temporary confinement, and looked over at what I had been carried here in. It was one of the bongo drums, a little bigger than the rest, with a side that opened out. It was probably built just for this trick.

I leaned over and felt Jed's pulse and then the pulse of his friend. They were both a little rapid but healthy. I considered sticking around to apologize, but then thought better of it. Both guys were probably so high that this zapping wouldn't even be a blip on their radar screens. Besides, everyone knows it's not cool to transport a chick to the woods in a carrier disguised as a bongo drum.

I jogged back toward the road and the party on Shangri-La. When I reached the edge of the woods, I slid my sandals off, laced them over my shoulder, and dropped down to the water's edge. The trees lining the shore of the pond side of the lake would keep me out of view. I skirted the lake, my feet sinking in the swampy beach. I envisioned leeches hanging off my toes like spaghetti noodles. It was gross, but being quiet was more important than being blood-sucker-free.

My plan was to make sure Sam and Jason were in the crowd, then sneak into the main lodge and up to the master bedroom. I estimated that I could be in and out in under five minutes. It was likely I had more time than that since whoever had an interest in my activities had already done their best to remove me from the island and wouldn't be expecting me back so soon, if at all.

I peered through a patch of weeping willows at the frenzy of the Romanov show, the bright light from the tiki torches making the scene vivid and ensuring my invisibility in the shadows. I couldn't see what was going on in the center, but people were seven deep all the way around. I spotted Sam leaning against a tree on the far side, her cigarette holder in place again, smoking and looking bored. It took me a while to find Jason, but it was worth the effort. He stood about fifty feet from me and on the other side of the crowd from Sam, looking uncomfortable as a bedecked Kennie leaned into him, her hand on his upper thigh.

She was talking animatedly, and every swing of her arms prom-ised to release one of the mammoth breasts shoved into the black rubber of her tank top. Her natural hair was buried under the red, green, and yellow braids of extensions, and she wore a tie-dyed skirt and Rasta sandals. Her red lipstick and green eye shadow comple-mented the cacophony of color. This was clearly her effort to attract a younger man, and I applauded it. No woman, no cry.

I took advantage of the distractions to sneak into the lodge through the darkened kitchen. I made my way up the main stairs, fishing in my purse for the skeleton key I had brought with me. I had the wild idea that it might work in a house as old as this one with all the original locks intact.

I reached the second floor and made my way to the massive master bedroom door, placing my hand on the cool crystal doorknob, and was startled when it swung open. "Hello?" I whispered. There was no answer, so I traded the skeleton key for the stun gun and my penlight and tiptoed in. Moonlight spilled across the carpet, illuminating a major mess and a minor carpentry project.

The bed was unmade and strewn with clothes, there were empty Coors Light bottles and two full ashtrays scattered on the floor, and all the furniture had been moved to the far side of the room. It looked like a rock band had stopped by, but that wasn't as shocking as the closet. The door had been taken off its hinges, and the interior was ripped apart. It was as if a hundred razor-toothed beavers had gone at it—the paneling was shredded, the wallpaper hung in strips, and there were holes punched in the Sheetrock.

This crude destruction had paid off, because in the back of the far right corner of the closet was an opening about three feet high and two feet wide. There was probably a switch that would have tripped the dwarf door to open, but a crowbar had done this dirty work. My heart was flirting with my stomach, and they both agreed I should get my ass in on this discussion and go home to relative safety. After all, I had already been made to disappear once tonight; I'm sure there were people around who wouldn't mind making that permanent.

However, I couldn't fight the feeling, like fizzy bubbles in my veins, that I was about to discover some huge treasure bigger than any rhinestone I had ever hidden. Instead of returning home to safety, I shined my flashlight in the space, dropping to my knees for a better view. My light revealed a shallow but long room that went farther than I could see. The architect who had planned this place must have devised it so that the room did not take enough space to be revealed from the outside but was large enough to house a major science project.

I leaned in closer to the opening, and my flashlight reflected off a metal structure that looked vaguely familiar. It took me a few seconds to place it. I had seen a similar contraption on an episode of *The Beverly Hillbillies* in which Jethro had been making moonshine. I guess I knew now how Whiskey Lake had gotten its name. Shangri-La had been built in the twenties, at the height of Prohibition.

The still didn't make sense, though. Regina had insisted that all the workers be fired after Shirly caught her messing in this closet, but had she been making moonshine? If she had traveled all the way from New York, it was unlikely she had the time or the means to establish an illegal liquor operation. And why would she come all the way to a remote lake in Minnesota to set it up? Surely, they could use the liquor out East.

I crouched down and squeezed myself into the hidden room. The floor had been dusty at one point, but a lot of footprints had flurried that. I ran my hands along the cool metal of the still and flashed my light up at the shelving that lined the back wall. There were hundreds of bottles stored on the shelves, and they all looked empty. Upon closer inspection, I could see that the still had been torn through as thoroughly as the closet to this room.

Immediately behind the still were two small white tanks that looked newer than everything else, along with some glass tubes like the ones we used in middle-school science class. One of the tanks had ANHYDROUS AMMONIA written on the side, and the other looked like a compact gas tank for a propane grill. I knew farmers used the ammonia around here to fertilize their corn, but I had no idea why it would be stored in this room next to a tank of gas for a grill. One thing was clear, though. Jason had not found what he was looking for in this room yet, or he would be gone.

Shirly had told me other guests had also lost their jewelry that summer long ago, not just Regina with her necklace. It seemed likely that all those stolen jewels were the treasure Jason was after. Regina must have been caught stealing or hiding jewelry when Shirly walked in on her in the closet. Now I wondered if she had also stumbled across the moonshining operation and whoever had been running it.

If the help had been running the still, firing them all would have given her free rein to hide her stolen goods in the secret chamber. Or, if the Addamses were moonshining, she may have blackmailed them after she stumbled across their operation, which would explain why they had sold the place shortly after her discovery and why they weren't mentioned in her obituary along with the Carnegies.

I knew my time was running out. Sam and Jason could come back at any minute, and I needed to find what they had missed. It looked like the two of them had gone over everything with a fine-toothed but greasy comb. Neither of them were neat people, though, and dirty people often don't acknowledge the world below knee level. I got on all fours and ran my hand along the bottom of everything—the still, the shelves, an old typewriter. I was almost ready to give up when I snagged some material underneath the shelf farthest from the entrance.

I pulled the purple silk bag out, amazed at the fabric's softness despite its obvious age. Inside the bag were four mothballs and a tied roll of leather about six inches long. I was pulling at the string securing it when I heard the door to the master bedroom open and then slam shut. My mouth and anus echoed the gesture.

I quickly switched off the flashlight, hoping its illumination hadn't been seen in the main room, and I shoved the silk-wrapped leather into my purse. I considered hiding based on my memory of this now-dark room, but I discarded that as stupid. It was only a matter of time until Jason and his mystery accomplice returned to this secret space, and judging by the two feet of Sheetrock and insulation and wood I had crawled through to get in, this space was soundproof. It would be pretty easy to do away with a body in here. After all, this secret chamber had gone undisturbed for over eighty years. I was in no hurry to rot in here for another eighty.

At least if I snuck back into the bedroom I could make a mad dash to the door, and yell for help if I didn't make it. Who knows? It might just be Sam out there, and I could take her down. I pulled out my stun gun and swore I'd name my first child after it if it got me out of here. This would all be a suspenseful bedtime story I'd tell little Z-Force some day.

I inched my way toward the opening, relieved when whoever was in the master bedroom flipped on a light. I could now make out the faint shapes of the stills and shelves. At the opening, I leaned toward the three-foot hole without peeking out and took stock of my surroundings.

"She's the goddamn mayor of the town, Sammie. What, am I supposed to be rude to her?"

I heard Sam take a drag off her cigarette. "How about keeping your tongue out of her throat? Would that be too damn rude?"

The corner of my mouth twitched. In my head, a childish voice sang, "Kennie and Jason, sittin' in a tree, kay-eye-ess-ess-eye-en-gee . . . "

Jason's voice became soft, pleading. "Baby doll, you know you're the only one I want to kiss. Come over here to Daddy."

I heard the bedsprings creak, followed by a deep, resigned sigh from over by the door. "I gotta pee first. Why don't you clean up some of this damn mess? You live like a pig."

The bathroom door opened. Seconds later, I heard what sounded like a racehorse emptying its bladder. Jason, meanwhile, began his version of cleaning. I heard the telltale zip of jeans and the sound of clothes hitting the floor. "Hurry up, baby! Little Jason ain't got all day."

The bathroom door opened again. "Baby, it don't take Little Jason longer than all of three minutes, so quit your bitchin'."

Score one for the lady. The light flicked off, and I waited until I heard the creaks of another body joining him on the bed. I slipped to my hands and knees and crawled out of the secret room and into the closet. The bed was to the right and out of sight of my spot, but I had a straight shot to the door, four feet to my left. I grimaced when the springs started squawking rhythmically, and I realized Sam wasn't lying about Jason's speed-racer love.

I fought the urge to stand up and run. If Jason saw me leaving the closet, he'd hunt me down to the ends of the earth. I sucked in a deep breath and forced myself out of the closet. The room was submerged in shadow, and I kept my head straight down to minimize movement and started crawling to the door. Out of the corner of my eye I saw Sam riding Jason like a ten-cent pony outside the drugstore, her fingernails scraping his back. I filed it all away under "Top Secret—Don't Open Again."

I kept my movements slow and disciplined and was at the front door in under a minute. I snaked up the wall and slid my hand toward the doorknob. It was crystal on this side too. I had my face to the wall with my back to the room, vulnerable. Then, the heaving on the bed stopped.

I panicked, ripped open the door, and ran. I heard yelling behind me, but I was taking the stairs four at a time and burst out the front door before Jason could yank his pants on. There was still a crowd outside, but it looked like the show was winding down. My goal was to get as far away as I could, and when I saw a clear path off the island, I ran. I got about ten feet before I heard a pop like a firecracker, and a fiery blow to the center of my forehead knocked me flat.

I heard someone yell, "It's a shooting! Somebody's been shot!"

People started screaming and moving back, and I lay there, paralyzed, feeling my head ache like a broken tooth. I had been shot. I experienced a warm trickle bleeding into one of my eyes, and I put my hand up, terrified. Why wasn't anyone helping me? I heard the crackle of a walkie-talkie, and then someone called 911 on a cell phone.

More than anything, I didn't want to touch the hole in my head, but I couldn't stop myself. I put my fingers on the spot about an inch above my eyebrows and was repulsed at the hard and wet blob protruding there. Were my brains coming out? Morbid curiosity won over prudence. I forced my hand back to the splash of flesh and gingerly lifted it off my head, tipping my eyes back so I could see it. The pain didn't get any worse, so I tried to focus on the blob. I blinked, and then blinked again. I was holding a squashed June bug. In my haste to escape Jason, I had collided with a flying beetle with such force that I had juiced it right on my own noggin.

I sat up shakily to tell the crowd the ambulance wouldn't be needed, that the dork who had almost drowned herself on a dead body yesterday had now just knocked herself silly on a June bug the size of a crow. That's when I realized that the crowd wasn't gathering around me, and the ambulance hadn't been called for my sake. Somebody really had been shot.

Brushing bug juice off my tender forehead, I pulled myself up and pushed through the mob circled around one of the last tiki torches still burning. The raucous sounds of partying had been replaced by the buzzing hum of confusion and panic. In the middle of the circle was the performer dressed as Tweedledee, and I saw that he had indeed been an adult, and was now an adult with a pool of blood gathering under his body. Kellie Gibson was by his side, holding his hand and asking him questions. The little guy wasn't moving.

I heard the ambulance charge up the narrow road to Shangri-La, and the crowd and I stepped back so the EMTs could access the fallen performer. While they were loading him onto the gurney, I turned to the guy next to me. "What happened?"

The man looked dazed, and he kept getting jostled by the crowd, both those trying to squeeze in for a better look and those trying to leave. "That crazy ringmaster shot him! He shot him and then disappeared into that black box! Jesus, what sort of show is this?"

I wondered the same thing. The happy island party was now a chaos of performers, police, and blood. I saw Chief Wohnt plow through the crowd and bark orders, but otherwise, the throng was a panicked blur. The paramedics cleared a path, and I realized that the carnival performers were melting into the dark. By the time the stretcher reached the ambulance, the only people left in the light of the torch were Battle Lake natives.

Why wouldn't the performers be gathered around one of their own? Were they after the ringmaster who had disappeared in the black box? If so, I had an inside edge. I knew where the ringmaster had "disappeared" to. I pushed through the people who were now trying to leave the island like lemmings. The police were cordoning off the area, and it looked like it was going to be a long night of questioning witnesses. I skirted into the shadows and left the way I had come, along the swampy beach side. I made it unnoticed to the edge of the woods where I had been dumped, stopping to worry momentarily about poison ivy. There was a bumper crop this year. Well, if I was going to get it, I already had it.

When I reached to the drop-off spot, I realized that I was too late. Jed and his fellow zappee must have recovered and left. There was a second bongo next to the one I had been carried here in, its front open to reveal an empty hiding spot. The murderous ringmaster had escaped, and Jason was no doubt on the prowl after a mysterious intruder. I wondered how well the ringmaster and Jason Blunt knew each other. There certainly had been an unusual amount of violence, real and staged, since the two had come to town. I would sleep at Gina's tonight, right after I reached a lighted area where I could look at what was in the purple silk I had lifted from the secret room.

TEN

THE ANTICIPATION WAS KILLING me, but I wanted to get far away from Jason and Shangri-La before I examined the scroll of leather in the purple fabric. I jogged to my car, locked all the doors, and drove to Ben's Bait in town. There, under the flickering glow of the parking-lot light, I unwrapped the cloth on the passenger seat and peeled the top layer back with all the anticipation of a lover opening a Valentine's Day gift. This movement released the scent of mothballs and revealed the tied, cracked leather inside. I unrolled this, too, and found a yellowed document within. The paper was so thick it felt handmade, and the blue-black ink had bled through when the message had been scratched on it decades earlier. The writing on the front was still clear, however, and it read:

Jvgu lbhe onpx gb gur xvffvat gerr jnyx frira fgrcf abegujrfg xarry 76 yrsg 87 evtug 88 yrsg.

My stomach dropped. I had been hoping to find a map with a big red X over a sparkly, Richie Rich drawing of diamonds. This was a message in a foreign code with regular numbers. I slapped my steering wheel in frustration. There was nothing more I could do with this tonight. Tomorrow, I would bring it to Battle Lake's resident wordsmith to see what he could puzzle out from it.

I woke up one hour past sunrise on Gina's faux-leather couch with a lump the size of a crab apple dead center on my forehead and a headache of Mardi Gras proportions. I stumbled into her bathroom, showered, and felt slightly worse. I needed coffee, ibuprofen, and a talk with Ron Sims, the county crossword-puzzle champion. He took words pretty seriously, and if he couldn't unscramble the puzzle I had found in the closet, no one could. One didn't get to run a newspaper without loving the language.

While I was in the newspaper's office, I needed access to the *Battle Lake Recall*'s archives to find out what the paper had to say about the diamond necklace and Mrs. Krupps back when it had all happened. A second visit to Shirly Tolverson might be in order as well. What I saw in the master bedroom the night before confirmed that he had done some judicious editing of his Shangri-La story. I hoped I could accomplish all this before I needed to open the library at ten.

I wrapped myself in a towel and stepped gingerly out of the bathroom, trying to hold my tender head completely still on my neck. Gina was sitting on the couch in the living room. "Hey, G, you have any ibuprofen?" It took me a second to realize that she shouldn't be home at this time of day; she should be three hours into her slave shift. Another beat later, I realized that she was crying.

"He's cheating."

"What?"

"Leif. He's cheating on me."

I sat down next to her and stretched my arm as far as it would reach around her plump shoulders. Her husband had always been the noncommittal type, but I had never taken him for a cheater. "How do you know?"

Gina stared at the floor, her face red and swollen. Her over-permed blonde hair was corralled into a scrunchie, and she wore a tattered brown bathrobe with old-fashioned grandma pajamas underneath. Her voice cracked when she spoke. "He told me. He said he needed to come clean with me because our relationship is so important."

I scowled at the weak logic of a guilty man. So he was an honest cheater? Give me a faithful liar any day. "I'm sorry, sweetie. Who's it with?"

"He wouldn't give me a name. Some ice-fishing hussy, I suppose. I knew I should have gone ice fishing with him when he asked. It's just so damn boring." She threw her head back, shaking tendrils of yellow hair loose from their tie, and sobbed like a three-year-old. I let her, even though every bellow dragged through my bug-bashed head like a rusty fishhook. When she calmed down, I asked her what she was going to do.

She sniffled on a bucket of snot and reached for the box of Kleenex. "What *can* I do, Mira? I love him. He's my husband, and we're together for better or worse."

Her words ignited a sudden white anger in me. That had been my mother's attitude during her entire tumultuous relationship with my father—he's my husband, and I have to stay. I had no time for this way of thinking. There was a misconception that bad people walked around with knives and guns, yelling expletives, and so were easy to distinguish from good people. The truth was that bad people looked just like the rest of us, and they could bring you a flower on your birthday or call you to find out how your day went or come to your basketball game. Then, when you were fooled into relaxing, they'd get drunk or have sex with a stranger after they'd pledged their heart, body, and mind to you. I believed that when someone showed their true colors, and those colors were black and gray, you needed to act accordingly and cut them out of your life.

I looked at Gina with her stringy blonde hair, runny nose, and puffy eyes. She didn't want to hear my theory on bad people. She wanted her husband to love her like mad. "Well, G, if you're going to stick it out, take advantage of your current position."

"Huh?" Another snort into her squelchy tissue.

"He's got his tail between his legs, so you take what you need right now. Get him to agree to marriage counseling and to take you out for a nice night at a fancy restaurant, if nothing else."

Her soggy green eyes stared into mine. "It can work, can't it, Mira? People can move past this stuff, right?"

I grimaced. "Anything is possible. Now I need some ibuprofen before my head rolls off and under the couch."

Gina provided the medicine, Sid and Nancy gave me a coffee and cinnamon scone on the house after they saw my green and purple forehead ("No shit. A June bug?"), and I met up with Ron Sims at the *Recall* office. It still smelled like ink and the walls were still tan, but something about the office hinted at excitement. This was a good time to own a newspaper in Battle Lake.

"Mira James! Just the person I was looking for. I've got two stories for you to write. Shoot, we might need a special edition!"

I could feel the ibuprofen kicking in and the caffeine stroking my serotonin levels nicely. Gina's sadness had painted a gray spot in me, but I could do this. "Fine, Ron. First, I need help with a puzzle. What language does this look like to you?"

He glanced over the top of his bifocals at the fragile paper and yanked it out of my hand. "English."

I pulled it back gently and tried to wipe off the glazed-donut fingerprints he had left. "In case you haven't noticed, I am somewhat familiar with the predominant language of North America. This isn't English."

"It's a cryptogram, James. Substitution cipher. Look at the numbers, syntax, and primary repetition of letters. Third-grade stuff. Now, if you want a real challenge, what you do is pull out the Sunday *New York Times* puzzle and settle back for a full, sweaty day of word wrestling. I remember—"

"Can you unjumble this?"

"Do fat men make the best lovers?"

Oh Christ! I hated trick questions. I copied the code onto his pink "While You Were Out" pad and returned the original to the silk wrap. "Just tell me what this says, okay?"

"Business before pleasure, James. Since you are the award-winning homicide writer, I want you to find out what you can about that midget who was shot last night at Shangri-La."

"I don't think they like to be called midgets, Ron."

"Well, make that part of your research. I need the scoop on him—his name, where he was from, how long he had been with the traveling theater, how he's doing—"

I wiped off my coffee mustache. "You mean he's still alive?"

"Last I heard over the police radio. He was alive when they brought him to Lake Region, anyhow. I need that article ASAP. Also, Chief Wohnt dropped off this press release. Make sure it's clean before we run it."

I looked at the paper Ron shoved in my hand. It was short and typed in an austere, sans serif font with zero formatting:

"Field drinking down 43%"
Otter Tail County teenagers are gathering and imbibing in local corn and soybean fields 43% less than they were a year ago. "We have only received three complaints about teenagers drinking in the fields, down from seven this time last year," according to Battle Lake Police Chief Gary Wohnt. "We attribute the decrease in outdoor, underage partying to the increase in random patrols, the DARE campaign, and the Olsen boys going off to college." The Battle Lake Police Department will continue to focus on fields as a source of trouble but will expand their efforts to parked cars, abandoned silos, and public beaches after hours.

Hallelujah. I needed to fact-check an article on field drinking, rural Minnesota's favorite youth sport, and write an article on a potentially murdered little person. Just another day at the office. "If I do this, you'll solve the puzzle? I'll throw in fresh hot scones from the Fortune for a full week."

He nodded and waved without looking up at me, his head buried in the puzzle and his glasses threatening to fall off his nose. "I need another recipe, too. Make it a dessert this time. Too many main dishes lately."

I nodded at his bald spot, pocketed the field-drinking press release, and headed to the back room. I knew the *Recall* had been around since the early 1900s, and I also knew Ron had paid big bucks to have a California-based document-scanning business convert all the microfiche archives to searchable PDF file format. This meant that I would be able to complete the background investigation I should have done on Shangri-La and its main players from the moment I had been handed the story.

I fired up the newspaper's Mac and searched editions from the 1920s. Back then, the newspaper only came out once a month, and it was mostly filled with crop information and sensationalistic stories on the dangers of immigrants and Indians. I was surprised to see a lot of pictures and ads, mostly for radios. An October 1923 ad promised to provide "a radio that can catch the waves out of Yankton, South Dakota!"

The August 1924 issue of the *Recall* featured a full page on the building of Shangri-La, but it didn't tell me anything new. It wasn't until the June 1929 issue that I hit pay dirt—a full-length article on the suspicious disappearance of jewelry at the Addamses' house. It listed these missing items: a Victorian lava cameo bracelet; two hematite intaglio rings; a coral, platinum, and diamond double-clip brooch; a black pearl sautoir; two sapphire, seven emerald, and twelve diamond rings; assorted diamond earrings; a diamond and emerald tiara; and a diamond pendant necklace. I whistled. That was quite a haul, and I didn't even know what a sautoir was. If the thief was half the stasher I was, Shangri-La was lousy with hidden bling.

I dug in my purse for paper to copy the list on. I shut down the computer and was out the door, hollering at Ron on my way past. "You call the minute you get that solved. Fresh scones . . ."

"Go! I'm not paying you to nag me!"

"Please. You couldn't get a high school student to work the fryer at the Dairy Queen for what you pay me. Call me, okay?"

"I'll call. If I don't get bogged down with more work, I'll have this solved within the hour."

And then my treasure hunt would truly begin, bringing me that much closer to tying up the loose ends and making Jason's life miserable.

ELEVEN

I STEPPED INTO THE blinding light of Main Street and pulled my gas-station-rack sunglasses over my eyes. It was nine-fifteen in the morning, and I wasn't sure where to go next. I wanted to talk to Shirly to ferret into what he had left out of his Shangri-La story, and I needed to interview Chief Wohnt, but I only had forty-five minutes until I was supposed to have the library unlocked and open for business. I shirked certain areas of my life, like forming relationships with other humans, and occasionally personal hygiene, but I had a strong work ethic, and the idea of not fulfilling my duties rankled.

I decided to visit the Senior Sunset first, because I could always phone Gary Wohnt for the information I needed. Shirly, however, needed to be talked to in person. I wanted to be able to read his face.

There is only one main street through Battle Lake, so everything is technically around the corner from something else. It would take me all of six minutes to walk to the nursing home. I counted six Ford and five Dodge pickup trucks on the way and walked past a crowd gathering in the First National Bank parking lot. Families had come out in droves to partake in and cheer on the turtle races, held every Tuesday during the summer months. A bank employee was hosing down the already-steaming pavement so the creatures didn't melt their mitts right into the black tar, and there were loads of brightly clothed kids painting numbers on the backs of the turtles.

I spotted Peyton standing alone off to the side of the crowd, wearing a bright pink sundress and matching hat, and I waved at her. She waved back with both skinny hands. I was not surprised to see her turtle-free. Technically, they were pretty dirty creatures with a tendency to pee like a river when alarmed. Leylanda would not allow Peyton to touch one of those. I was actually surprised Leylanda had retracted her meat hooks far enough to let Peyton stand in the parking lot out of smothering distance. She must be nearby.

I swiveled my head, looking for her, and was shocked to see her talking animatedly with Jason. The sight of him made me feel like I had cement hardening in my stomach. He had buzzed off his hair between last night and now, and the severe cut drew attention to the slant of his dark, restless eyes. I instinctively ducked behind a Ford F-150 and watched the two interact. Leylanda was laughing and he was nodding at her, ogling her boobs whenever she'd toss her head back to giggle. I hadn't been aware that they knew each other, though it made sense because they were about the same age and had both grown up in Battle Lake. I wondered if the two were hooking up. They didn't seem to have much in common on the surface, but I knew Jason could be charming when he wanted to, and I guessed Leylanda was lonely. She was divorced, her husband long gone, and Jason considered himself single no matter who he was seeing, so I suppose the two were free to date.

I was too far away to hear what they were talking about, but I saw their faces change as they both glanced toward Jason's crotch. They must have been reacting to a noise, because he pulled his cell phone out of his pocket and put it to his ear. He winked at Leylanda and turned away. I was the only one who saw how dark and still his face became as he continued the conversation. Abruptly, he jerked the phone from his ear, fished in his front pants pocket, pulled out a few green bills, and handed them to Leylanda, who was standing directly behind him. He pointed across the street at Granny's Pantry. Leylanda made a motion toward Peyton, who was watching the turtle races hypnotically.

Jason waved his hand in an "It'll be fine" manner and walked over to Peyton, effectively dismissing her mother. Leylanda watched him uncertainly, looked back at Granny's Pantry, and back at Peyton. She squeezed the money in her hand and walked to the candy store, going as fast as she could without looking like she was running.

Jason, for his part, strode stiffly to the rear of the parking lot. The kiddie crowd cheered as the first turtle crossed the line, and I saw Peyton break out of her trance and look around. She didn't see her mom, so she skipped over to Jason, who had his back to her and the crowd as he continued his animated phone conversation. Meanwhile, Leylanda ran into and popped out of Granny's in record time. She must have grabbed whatever was closest to the door, thrown her money at the cash register, and dashed out.

That four seconds was probably the longest Peyton had ever been out of Leylanda's sight. As soon as Peyton spotted her mom hurrying around the side of the bank, she ran to her and grabbed at the bag in her hand. I couldn't see Peyton's face, but I imagine she was miserably disappointed when she pulled out the Red Delicious apple. I didn't even know Granny's sold fruit. It should be illegal for a candy and ice cream shop to sell healthy things. Is nothing sacred?

Jason clicked his phone shut, and even from my hidden location I could feel his icy rage. Apparently, whoever had called Jason had given him some very bad news. This was my cue to flee the scene. I curved my shoulders and tried to turn myself inside out so he wouldn't see me, and I strode swiftly away from the bank. I was a block from the turtle races and in sight of the nursing home when his brawny hand clamped down on my shoulder and made me jump like a squirrel.

"Hello, Mira."

I shrugged his paw off and tried to walk away, but he wrapped his arm around my waist and led me behind Walvatne's Dentistry in a vicious two-step. I looked back at the turtle races, but no one was facing our direction save a wistful-looking Leylanda. I considered yelling, but I didn't think Jason would hurt me in public and I didn't want to scare the kids.

"I saw you made it to the show last night," he whispered into my ear.

I pushed myself away from him, and he let me go now that we were out of sight. "I saw you, too. It looked like you and Kennie were having a blast. Are you going steady, or was it just a heat-of-the-moment thing?"

He swelled up like a premenstrual salt lick, and his fingers twitched at his sides. Then, just like that, he was calm. "Yeah, that was pretty funny. I'm glad the guys didn't see me with her. I'd never hear the end of it, being hit on by a big nasty skank like Kennie Rogers."

I was speechless. Suddenly, I was talking with the easygoing Jason that Sunny called one of her best friends. Hello, bipolar.

"Say, Mira, funniest thing." He laughed here to illustrate his point, a warm, companionable laugh that made my lips twitch against my better judgment. "Someone took something very special from me last night. Could you help me find it?"

I was certain Jason hadn't seen me clearly last night when I fled his room, so I had nothing to lose by acting helpful now. "Sure, Jason. Meet me at the library in about half an hour to tell me how I can help. Really though, man, I need to go."

I turned to leave and he wrenched the hobo purse I was still carrying off my shoulder. I grabbed at it, but he was too quick. "Golly, Mira, I don't think you need to go yet." His tone was the same, but his eyes were sharp and black, his pupils eerily swollen in the light.

The purple-silk-wrapped message was on the top, and he grabbed it easily and tossed my brown crocheted purse to the ground. "You're a real pal, Mira. Thanks! I've been looking everywhere for this!" He punched my shoulder hard enough to knock me to the ground and laughed sharply.

As he walked away, he said, "Ignore the message I left at your place. We're cool now."

I watched his broad back turn the corner. Tears came to my eyes as I thought about my cat and dog, vulnerable, spending the night alone at my house. If Jason had hurt Tiger Pop or Luna, I was going to Z-Force zap him until he spoke French.

"Are you okay, honey?"

I turned quickly at the voice and wiped the tears from my eyes. "Hi, Mrs. Berns. Yeah, I just fell on the ground."

"No shit. Pretty hard to fall anywhere else." She helped me up and brushed the dirt off me. "How come you're not opening up the library?"

"I don't feel very well, Mrs. Berns." I was grateful that she ignored my tears.

"Well, give me the damn keys. I'll open her up."

"Really?"

"Honey, I raised twelve children, ran a farm and a business, and sewed all my own clothes. I think I can boot up a computer and scan some codes."

I had no doubt. However, being fertile and good with a needle didn't necessarily translate into good public relations skills. Unfortunately, I didn't see any other option if the library was going to be opened on time. I handed her the keys and considered hugging her, but I needed to get back to my place and make sure Tiger Pop and Luna were alive and healthy. I jogged back to my car, feeling tightness in the knee I scraped when Jason pushed me.

I sped the whole way home and up my driveway and ran into the house. There was not a clean surface to be found, and the house smelled like sewage and rotten fruit. The bookshelf was on its side, books ripped apart and pages scattered. The kitchen cupboards had been ripped open, and the food inside of them had been dumped or tossed. My bedroom was the worst. The quilt and pillows were shredded, and my drawers and closets were pulled apart, clothes scattered and torn everywhere. The bathroom wasn't as bad, but in the middle of the extra-large tub was a bear-sized poop. Jason wasn't lacking for fiber in his diet.

He clearly knew, or had assumed, it was me who was in the hidden room last night, and he must have had an idea of what he was looking for. I wondered if Jason would be as disappointed with the code in the purple cloth as I was.

"Meow."

Really. That's how he said it. I ran into the laundry room and saw him stretching in a sunbeam. I buried my face in his fur and grabbed some catnip to reward him for being alive. Then, out of paranoia, I dashed out to my garden and was relieved to see it was untouched. When Luna loped out of her shaded house to walk me to the garden, I finally relaxed. Jason thought he was getting at me, but he hadn't even recognized the things that mattered. Both animals still had dishes full of food, but I got them fresh water and sat outside with them for a half an hour, telling them what had transpired the past twelve hours and how happy I was that they were all right.

Afterward, I stopped just short of calling Mrs. Blunt to tell her that her youngest son had shat in my tub. I had no doubt she would give him an earful, but I wanted to do some more permanent damage. I cleaned up the mess in the house and used a plastic-wrapped dustpan and broom to relocate the poop to the toilet. When it was all said and done, my place looked as good as new, except now I had more garbage than belongings. I would need to add grocery and clothes shopping to my to-do list.

I packed up Luna and Tiger Pop and dropped them off at Gina's empty house. We wouldn't be going home until Jason was behind bars. I felt in my bones that he was connected to the shooting at Shangri-La last night, but I needed time to prove it. That meant I had to find the missing jewelry before he did, because he would be gone once he had it in hand.

After I made sure my kitty and foster dog were comfortable, I went to the library to check on Mrs. Berns. She had set up a table in front where she was selling kisses for a quarter (or free to anyone who signed up for our newsletter) and giving books away to anyone who could guess her age and weight. Fortunately, the library was slow on Tuesday mornings, even with all the contest-related business in town, so I decided to run over to the nursing home before I relieved her.

Solving the mystery of the missing jewelry had taken on a new immediacy now that it was affecting my home life. I blew into the lobby, ignoring the nurse at the front desk, the smell, and the drooping people in wheelchairs lining the halls like skin garlands. I was happy to find Shirly in his room reading the newspaper.

"Well, hello, Ms. James!"

"Mira."

"Well, hello, Mira! I hear there's some excitement going down in the real world, most notably at Shangri-La." His eyes twinkled.

"You heard right." I sized him up. He was in the same position on his bed, but now he was wearing navy blue carpenter pants and a cream-colored polo. His hair and smile were still impeccable. He actually looked quite dashing, but I caught a mischievous glint in his eyes that I had overlooked at our last meeting.

"Shirly, remember when you told me that you caught Dolores Krupps snooping in the master bedroom closet at Shangri-La?"

"Regina. Regina Krupps."

He had known her first name. When I first interviewed him, he acted like he wasn't even sure about her last name. "Oh, that's right. What do you think she was doing in the closet?"

"If you ask me, she was hiding the jewelry she had been stealing since she got there."

I wasn't the only one who thought she was the thief. "Why would she go all the way up there to hide it? Wouldn't she be worried the Addamses would look in their own closet and come across it?"

Shirly appeared to consider this for the first time. He was the picture of thoughtful introspection. "You might be right. Maybe she was just stealing from them."

"And do you think she came across the secret room with the bootlegging operation set up in it while she was *stealing* the jewels or while she was *hiding* them?"

Shirly tensed, and then he laughed. "You got a nosy streak the size of a lake. How'd you know about the moonshine?"

"I checked out the secret room last night. The setup is still there."

"Still there, eh? I wondered about that. The room was built around it, you know. Prohibition was the scourge of the twenties, made honest men do dishonest things. The architect who built Shangri-La had a lucrative side business going building those rum rooms."

I followed this information with a natural conclusion. "So the Addamses had him build a still into a secret room in their summer place."

Shirly smiled in a faraway manner. "No, they didn't. The architect was tired of getting a little money here and there for the rum rooms. He wanted one of his own. He knew that the Addamses wouldn't be around much, and their house was going to be big enough to accommodate a secret room. All the workers knew about the room, but the Addamses never did. During the summer season, the rum room was untouched. When the Addamses boarded the place up for the winter, the distilling of spirits would commence."

That crossed one theory off the list. "I thought maybe Regina had all you guys fired and was blackmailing the Addamses because she found out about the still."

"She found the rum room, all right. Purely by accident. I caught her with a handful of jewels, digging for some more in the master bedroom closet. When I walked in on her, I scared her so bad that she accidentally tripped the wire that opened up the room.

"I told her right off that the Addamses didn't know about the moonshine. They were the nicest people and didn't need the trouble that would bring on them. Mrs. Krupps said that it would be our little secret—I wouldn't tell anyone about her stealing and she wouldn't tell anyone about the liquor."

"So she lied to you?"

"Not technically. She never told the Addamses about the rum room. I imagine it was too perfect a hiding place for her booty. She did tell them that she caught me stealing, though, and that she thought the other workers were in on it. Now, you remember I wasn't more than a boy. I was ashamed to be thought a thief, but I knew the Addamses would treat me better with that crime than the police would treat me as a moonshiner."

I grimaced. "I think I know what happens next. The Addamses fire you, they reimburse the guests for the stolen jewelry, but jewelry keeps disappearing as long as Regina Krupps is staying at Shangri-La."

Shirly nodded his head. "Jewelry's not all. Mrs. Krupps's husband disappeared, too. Those of us who got fired joked that she stole him and hid him in the secret chamber along with the rest of her ill-gotten gains."

I shuddered at the thought. I was pretty sure I would have noticed a dead body, but I suppose one could have been hidden in one of the larger vats of the still. "So why did a rich lady need to steal?"

"You got me. I think it was one of those compulsions. She wasn't well in the head. She spent a lot of time arguing with herself when she thought no one was listening, and I once saw her hiding acorns in her mouth just like a chipmunk. It was out back of the third servant's cabin. That woman was a loon, but only sometimes. When she wasn't loopy, she was wicked smart. That's the worst kind of crazy if you ask me, but back then, they called her 'eccentric.'"

It occurred to me that all of us were crazy sometimes. I was thinking specifically of the whole year I spent convinced that Jimmy Page was trying to contact me through hidden messages in Led Zeppelin's fourth album, but I kept that to myself. "Why'd the Addamses sell Shangri-La?"

"The thievery got to be too much. The police were even brought in, but of course no one ever found anything. Mrs. Krupps was hiding the stolen loot right under everyone's noses and never had to transport any of it. People got to talking about the place being haunted. The Addamses got too frustrated and pulled up roots and built elsewhere. Somewhere on the upper Mississippi, if memory serves."

"And the stolen jewelry?"

"Never found."

"Think she took it with her back to New York?"

"The police were pretty thick around Battle Lake at the end. A smart woman would have hidden the jewelry and come back later for it."

My thoughts exactly. And all the evidence I had so far indicated that Mrs. Regina Krupps had been very smart, if a little bit crazy, and for some reason hadn't returned for her jewelry. It was still in the neighborhood. I couldn't wait to find out what Ron had to tell me about the secret message I had left with him.

TWELVE

THE BATTLE LAKE POLICE Department was located on my way back to the library, and I ducked in. This was the second time in two months that I had voluntarily visited the PD, which was a record for a small-town girl. When you grow up in an area where violent crime consists of cow tipping and vandalism is just a fancy word for toilet-papering a house, you get used to cops being more of an obstacle to a good buzz than a real necessity.

Chief Wohnt was at his desk in the front room. Actually, his desk *was* the front room, with a handful of chairs and filing cabinets thrown around to distract from the faux-wood paneling. He looked up when I entered and looked right back down.

"Hello, Chief."

"I suppose you found another body." He stated this as fact, as if it were the natural order of things.

"Nope." I was determined to remain perky. "No body. Nobody. Ha!"

The Chief was immune to perkiness. He pulled out a pot of Carmex from his chest pocket and slathered it on his lips. Clearly, he had been trained in the art of mind games and was trying to get me to blurt out a confession for some unnamed crime by creating an uncomfortable silence. I was all over that.

"Anyhow, Chief. You know that little guy who was shot last night?"

Silence.

"By the ringmaster from that Romanov Traveling Theater group?"

He pulled out a pack of Big League Chew and stuffed the pink shreds into his cheek, careful not to mess his shiny lips. I caught a whiff of my favorite childhood brand of bubble gum and was reminded of simpler days when the big excitement in my life had been staying up to watch *Mutual of Omaha's Wild Kingdom*. Would Jim get impaled by the waterbuck or have a goofy run-in with the vervet monkey? Tune in next week.

"Look, you know who I'm talking about. The extra-short guy who was killed by the ringmaster at Shangri-La last night. I have a right to this information as a public citizen and as a reporter." I hoped this was true, and I hoped I could goad him into replying.

"He wasn't killed."

"Thank you. Where can I find him?"

The Chief leaned back in his chair and switched his gum wad to the other cheek. "When you find out, you tell me."

"What?"

"He was brought to Lake Region Hospital last night. Somewhere between the ambulance and the hospital room, he disappeared. We have an APB out for him and the shooter."

"You what? You lost a gunshot victim? What about the Romanov troupe?"

"Left town."

"I can understand losing the little guy, but a whole theater company?"

The Chief blinked quietly at me and returned to his paperwork.

"You know, maybe you should spend less people power on raiding fields and more on catching possible murder victims."

No reply.

"Say, speaking of field drinking, is it true that it's down 43 percent in the Battle Lake area?"

"Yup."

"Thanks." I left more frazzled than I had arrived, the information of the past three days swirling in my head like floaters in the toilet. Shirly confirmed that Regina Krupps had been stealing jewelry from Shangri-La guests back in the twenties. He also said Mr. Wilson Krupps, her husband, had disappeared during the same time and that the Addamses never knew about the moonshining.

Fast-forward to today. I knew Jason was violent and that he was rooming with Samantha Krupps, who used to be a nurse for Regina and may or may not have been related to her. They were in town and searching for treasure. All the anecdotal evidence I had accumulated indicated that Regina had hidden her stolen stash in this area and never returned for it, and that she had told Samantha, who had told Jason, where to look for it.

At the same time they're looking for the stolen jewelry, the *Star Tribune* runs a contest to find Regina's missing necklace that likely had never been lost in the lake. Finally, a fake dead body is planted in the waters in front of Shangri-La and a man is shot by his theatrical boss, and then he and the ringmaster disappear before anyone can question them. I wasn't a big believer in coincidence, and Jason had brought too much to town with him.

I went to the *Recall* office to find out how Ron's detective work was coming. He was on the phone, a string of cherry licorice in his mouth and his wife on his lap. She wore a Walkman and was writhing and humming. He looked crabby.

I tried waiting until either the phone call or his wife finished, but both looked committed to the long haul. "Ron," I hissed.

He waved dismissively in my direction.

"Ron! Did you finish that thing I left?"

He glared. "I'm on the phone!"

"Okay, I'll go. Just tell me if you finished that puzzle."

He shooed me with his hand again and took a big bite of licorice. His wife bent over and took a slow bite off the other end. Nothing was worth this. I turned to go.

"Wait, Mira!" Ron put his hand over the mouthpiece and handed the rest of the licorice to his wife. "That little guy who was shot last night called, said he had a story to tell. I told him to call you at the library since you were on this one. Why aren't you at the library?"

"Because I'm trying to write the stupid stories you've assigned me!" Ron didn't hear me. He had already gone back to his phone call. I closed the door and jogged up the street to the library. This could be the break I was waiting for to connect Jason with something that could get him in real trouble. I just hoped I hadn't missed the phone call.

When I barreled into the library, I found it empty except for the books and Mrs. Berns soul-kissing the middle-aged, unmarried owner of the Trim and Tan. "Mrs. Berns! Did anyone call while I was out?"

She was oblivious to the outside world, but Tony pulled away and looked embarrassed. He tried to make like I had just caught them in the middle of a conversation. "Yes, I'd love to receive the library newsletter. And you have my name and address right down there. Very good. Good. Okay then, bye!" He stumbled out the door, tripping over his own feet.

Mrs. Berns wiped her mouth and smiled at his retreating figure. "He'll be back."

"Mrs. Berns, did anyone call for me?"

"A few people. Ya know, you're a very popular girl." She winked at me and doddered toward the door, her purse in hand.

"Mrs. Berns, did they say who they were?"

She fluffed her apricot hair and pursed her lips. "I'm sure they did, dear. It would be rude not to." She continued to the door.

I tried to keep my voice level. "Who called for me and what did they have to say, Mrs. Berns?"

She sighed in a put-upon way. "A Wicket W. Warrick called. Said you'd want to talk to him because he had a good story to tell. He said he'd call back tomorrow about the same time, and if you weren't here, you'd be shit outta luck. I didn't care for him one bit. That's no way to talk to a lady."

Warrick must have been the little guy. "Who else called?"

"Gina, that nice girl married to that good-for-nothing Hokum boy. She said she'd talk to you tonight. And I think that was it."

"Thank you, Mrs. Berns. And I appreciate you opening up the library for me. That was really nice of you."

"That's a ten-four, good buddy." Mrs. Berns set off the book alarms as she went out the door, but I didn't stop her. I figured a couple paperbacks were a fair trade for helping a friend out of a jam.

I sat down heavily in my swiveling front-desk chair. Until Ron broke the code or Wicket W. Warrick called to let me know why he'd been shot and then disappeared, there was nothing to do but wait. I was a terrible waiter, and I was too antsy to do anything productive, which left me in mental purgatory. I started doodling on the scrap paper at the front desk with one of the standard-issue library mini-pencils.

I started out with a rainbow and clouds, and then I sketched a cool lake underneath, full of one-dimensional fish smiling at each other. Two fish seemed to be of the same species, so I drew a little hat and tuxedo on one and a wedding dress on the other. I added a clam to officiate and drew a large heart around the love trio.

The drawing irritated an itch that had been in my brain since I had talked to Shirly that morning. I worried it out of the back of my head. What had really happened to Wilson Krupps, husband to Regina? Her obituary said he had preceded her in death, but Shirly made it sound like he had fallen off the face of the earth. I went back online to the *Niagara Gazette* website where I had found Regina's obituary.

The newspaper had contact information listed, so I called and asked if they had any more info on the Krupps family other than what was listed in the recent obituary. The woman I was talking to was friendly but didn't have the information. "Regina Krupps was pretty famous around here, but I don't remember her husband. You say he was mentioned in the obituary?"

"Yes. It says he preceded her in death. I'm doing a local article on her philanthropy, and I wanted to know how involved her husband was."

"Well, I'll need to have someone call you back. Could you spell your name for me, please?"

I dreaded spelling my name over the phone. I had some disturbing disorder where I was hellishly tempted to utter vulgar matches for the letters—M as in "masturbate," I as in "intercourse," et cetera. I didn't know what that was. I was thinking of doing some volunteer work so if I ever gave in to my compulsion, I'd have a karmic buffer. "Mira James, just like it sounds. Thank you so much for your time!"

"Not a problem. You should get a call back soon."

This left me with more waiting, so I went online to find a dessert recipe for my column in the *Recall*. There was a suggestions envelope taped on my desk, but the only recipes I got in there required cream of mushroom soup (even the desserts), and I wasn't going to stoop that low. The Internet had so far provided me with great ideas. My two favorites on this current search were Snowman's Balls and Barbecued Spiced Bananas. The first called for two cups of graham crackers, one cup of powdered sugar, two tablespoons cocoa, one cup of chopped nuts, a quarter cup coconut syrup, a quarter cup brandy, and shredded coconut. You stick it all in a bowl except for the coconut, mix it up, and roll it in the coconut shreds. Voila! Snowman's balls.

It was out of season, though, and not as easy to make as the spiced bananas, offered to me courtesy of the website "Sancho's Disturbing Recipes of the Eerie Past." To prepare these, one peels a banana and places it in double-thickness heavy-duty aluminum foil. Then, one brushes it with lemon juice, sprinkles it generously with brown sugar, dusts it with cinnamon or nutmeg, and dots it with margarine. Finally, the tin foil is puckered tightly around this tropical surprise, which is then placed on the grill for seven to eight minutes. It sounded delicious and looked completely phallic, especially, I imagined, when served with hot dogs, which was going to be my recommendation. There's nothing to promote family togetherness like a whole plateful of penis-shaped food. Maybe next week I would pay homage to a different body part in my recipe column.

Recipe downloaded and e-mailed to Ron, I pretended to dust and tried to keep my mind busy. Fortunately, the library crowd began to pick up after lunchtime. There was a lot of talk about the people arriving in town to search for the black box the *Star Tribune* had planted. Apparently, a team of professional divers was camping at Glendalough State Park, and one woman said she heard Channel 5 out of Alexandria was going to run a story on the contest on tonight's newscast.

I had given up on finding the box the *Star Tribune* had planted as soon as I realized the real diamonds were still around. Having a redneck poop in my tub had also reprioritized my life for the moment. Regardless, it was kind of exciting to think that someone was going to find the box and that we'd have some cosmopolitan and energetic people in Battle Lake.

I was surprised that I was feeling slightly territorial, and it wasn't just because I was worried the *Star Tribune* was going to scoop me again. I wanted a local to find the box, and I wanted the town to put on a nice face for the world. There really were a lot of good people living in Battle Lake, and I didn't want strangers making fun of them. That was my job.

Sal Heike was making small talk with me and rifling through a pile of books on organic gardening and filing for bankruptcy when the phone rang. I excused myself to answer it.

"Is this Mira James?"

"Yes, it is. What can I do for you?"

"Hi! I'm Elizabeth Tang with the *Niagara Gazette*. You called looking for information on Wilson Krupps?"

"Oh yeah. Thanks for calling me back! I'm writing an article on the Krupps family here in Battle Lake, Minnesota. I have all the info I need, but there is one discrepancy. My sources indicate Mr. Krupps disappeared sometime in the 1920s. The obituary you guys ran three weeks ago said he died. Do you know which it is?"

"Probably both. I dug up what we have on them when I got the message you called. There isn't much, but we do have an article that ran when the Niagara County Center for the Arts was built in 1940. Although Mr. Krupps is named as a contributor for the Center, it reads, 'He was last seen in Otter Tail County, Minnesota, in the summer of 1929. Mr. Krupps is believed dead, and Mrs. Krupps dedicates this building to the loving memory of him.'"

"Wow. So he might be alive?"

"Maybe, but I doubt it. Mrs. Krupps was 104 when she died last month, and her husband was likely the same age as her or older when they married. If he didn't die in Minnesota in the twenties, he's probably died since of natural causes. Why the interest in him again?"

"Oh, it's not him so much. I want to make sure my article on Regina is accurate before I run it. I'll just mark him down as deceased."

"That's what we did in the obituary. It made the most sense." She hesitated for a moment. "That Mrs. Krupps was quite the woman. I bet you didn't have any trouble finding dirt on her!"

"You got that right!" I was bluffing, of course. "You guys have the same experiences with her out there?"

"Oh yes. She's a legend around here. She was pretty high profile because of all the money she came into when she married Wilson Krupps. It was a classic rags-to-riches story. Too bad she was crazy."

"You got that right! Kooky Krupps, that's how they refer to her around here."

"I believe it. That lady was as crazy as the day is long. One day she'd be at a public event as nice and normal as apple pie, and the next day she'd be calling the local radio station complaining about the government poisoning her water. I imagine a psychiatrist would have pronounced her schizophrenic, if she'd ever gone to one."

"No doubt."

"Send me a copy of your article when you're done. I'd be interested in reading it."

Great. Now I'd have to fabricate an article and send it off. "You got it. Thank you for your time, Ms. Tang. You've been helpful!"

"Not a problem. We writers need to stick together. Let me know if I can be of any more help."

"Will do." I discarded all the lies I had just told and kept the warm feeling I got at being called a writer long after we hung up. Well, I wanted to anyhow, but Kennie Rogers rumbled in and chilled the warm right out of me.

Her drugstore cologne preceded her like acid rain. As usual, her face was overly made up, but her hair extension distracted from that. She had perched a frizzy bun made out of curls two shades darker than her own hair color on the high point of her head. The hairpiece reminded me of a nesting chipmunk, but maybe that was because of the lime green Alvin and the Chipmunks beach cover-up she was wearing above her platform rainbow flip-flops. "Mira James, I do declare you know how to pick 'em! That Jason Blunt was quite the kisser. And what in the name of Dixie happened to your head?"

I felt my forehead, worried, and rubbed across my June-bug goose egg. I had in point of fact forgotten about it. "I ran into a bug."

"Well, sweetie, you don't have to tell the truth, but you can lie better than that. Now, about that job last night." I reached for my purse.

"Not necessary. I couldn't charge you for all the fun I had on Shangri-La. It wouldn't be decent. I consider kissing a handsome man volunteer work to be conducted for the greater good of Kennie." She pulled icy pink lipstick out of her bag and delicately applied it to her lips and their greater surroundings. "I do have a favor I need in return, though, honey."

My stomach tensed. Why was I thinking that it'd be a lot cheaper to pay cash?

"I need you to babysit my nephew tonight."

Whew. "I didn't know you had any brothers or sisters."

"Okay, if you're going to play it that way. He's not my nephew, he's a friend of Gary Wohnt's in town from Alaska. We're supposed to show him a good time tonight, and I don't want to entertain the dolt all night long. It seems like a fair trade, considering what I did for you last night. You in?"

I was so not in that it was ridiculous. "I'd love to Kennie—really, really love to spend the night with you, Gary Wohnt, and some strange guy from Alaska—but I have to work tonight."

"Sweetie, where y'all have to work tonight?" Her voice was peaches and cream and arsenic.

"Newspaper work."

"Give me that phone." She grabbed the handset and dialed Ron before I knew what was happening. Of course he said I didn't have to work tonight, as long as I got my articles in before deadline.

"We're set, darlin'. I'll pick you up at seven. I heard at the Turtle Stew that you're staying at Gina's, right? Look pretty. Oh, and Ronnie said he won't have time to get to your puzzle code until tomorrow." And she was out the door, leaving me in her hurricane wake.

I was shocked. No, I was horrified. This turn of plans was making a turd in the tub look like pennies from heaven. I wondered if I could get Mrs. Berns to pinch-hit for me tonight, too. Sigh. I probably could, but Kennie had done me a favor last night, and I did owe her one. I'd pay the piper. At least I wouldn't have to worry about being assaulted by Jason for the night.

THIRTEEN

Both Gina's husband and I were still staying at the Hokum house. If I hadn't needed a place, I imagine he would have been on the couch, but as it was, they slept in the same bed. When I returned to Gina's and told her about my "date," she laughed until she had hiccups. She even called Leif at work to tell him about it. I could hear him hooting over the phone from across the room. Apparently my dating woes lightened their marital strife. Gina made me swear to wake her up and tell her about the night no matter how late it went.

"Oh, this won't be going late."

"Oh, I don't know. He might be your magical mystery man."

"Ha! I don't envision Kennie and Gary Wohnt being the garnish on my plate of love. In fact, I need to get myself repulsive and quick to keep this short and sweet. Or just short and short."

"Want me to curl your hair?"

"No."

"Want to borrow my blue eye shadow?"

"No."

"Can I come spy on you?"

"No."

"Well, then I'll just ding around my house until you get home."

"Fine."

She sat next to me, facing the window looking out on the street, and we both waited in relative silence, punctuated only by her sporadic bursts of giggling. I found small comfort in the fact that my misery was distracting her from hers.

I was almost relieved when Kennie pulled up in her trademark pink two-door 1967 Plymouth Barracuda fastback with a V-8 and roaring glass packs (in case anyone wasn't paying attention). Getting this evening done and over with was better than waiting for it to happen, because there was no way anything could be as bad as I was imagining.

"Yoo-hoo!" Kennie waved her hand out the car window and honked.

Gina pulled me up and shoved me out, giving my butt a good pinch on the way. Halfway to the car, I saw the passenger-side door of the car open and Gary Wohnt step out. He looked away from me. Another head popped out, this one gray and moist-looking. As my date turned toward me, I guessed he was about five-foot-ten, maybe fifteen years older than my twenty-nine, with a broad, pork-white face accented by large, square glasses. He was stout but not overweight, and was wearing a brand-new wife beater and shorts. Except for his jowls, he was unremarkable. Maybe this wouldn't be heinous. At least he appeared to have teeth.

That's when his hand came out from behind his back. He held a wrist corsage laid out in a plastic box like a body in a coffin. Gina slammed the house door shut behind me, and I could hear her laughing so hard she fell over on the other side of it.

"Hello, little lady. I'm Ody."

"Hi, Ody." I gestured at the pink and blue flower mound. "Is that for me?"

"I don't see any other pretty girls around here. May I?" He slipped the carnations out of the plastic to-go case, stretched the elastic band, and offered it up to me. I let him put it on. What did I have to prove? My only concern was that it didn't house a tracking device that would prevent me from being able to flee later.

"Thanks, Ody."

"Thank you for—"

Kennie laid on her horn. "Save it for when she's drunk, Ody. I'm hungry!"

I hopped in and sat behind Kennie. Ody crawled in next to me, drowning us both in the spicy-sweet smell of Old Spice. "Where're we eating, Kennie?"

"Halverson Park for a picnic. Gary thought it would be romantic." Kennie squeezed his knee, and I squeezed my throat to keep the bile down.

I made a stab at friendliness. "So, Chief Wohnt, since you're off duty, I guess I can call you Gary?"

The Chief glared holes through the windshield. He wasn't returning Kennie's affection, either. The two of them never acted like they were dating when they were in public, though the whole town assumed they were a couple because they were always together. I wondered if Chief Wohnt would let his guard down tonight.

And speaking of chiefs, I was happy to be spending the first part of the night at the feet of Chief Wenonga, my favorite twenty-three-foot-tall fiberglass Indian. The effigy had been erected at Halverson Park in 1979 as a way to "honor" the original settlers of Battle Lake, the Ojibwe Indians. The real Chief Wenonga was the Ojibwe leader who had given Battle Lake its name over a hundred and fifty years ago. This fiberglass Chief Wenonga was a tall girl's wet dream. He was dark and steely-eyed in an alpha male kind of way, with a washboard stomach and a nice package.

I had been having adult dreams starring Chief Wenonga for a few weeks now. I suppose Freud would attribute this attraction to unattainable fiberglass men to having lost my father in my teens, but for me, it was all about hope. Some people longed for Brad Pitt. I had Chief Wenonga. It's only crazy if you tell someone else.

Ody hadn't said two words since Kennie had scolded him outside Gina's, and that was fine by me. Kennie parked the car, and we all piled out at the Halverson parking lot and filed to the lone picnic table and rusty swing set near Chief Wenonga's base. I winked up at him. He pretended he didn't see me. It was our game.

"Hope you like smoked fish!" Ody smiled and straddled a bench as Kennie unloaded the picnic basket. "Brought it all the way from Alaska!"

I liked smoked fish about as well as I liked smoked toes, but I could do the small-talk game. I was actually a little curious about what sort of person would be friends with Gary Wohnt. "What do you do in Alaska?"

Ody's pale face grew serious. "I'm a peace officer, just like my good friend and fellow rascal, Gary Wohnt. I do God's work in God's country."

"What do you do for fun?"

"That's where it gets interesting." He shifted his weight so he could lean toward me, his hands up like the goalposts on a football field. "I'm one of those guys who likes to live for the moment, see?"

"Sure."

"Yeah. Some people say, 'This is my life. What am I going to do with it?' I say, 'This is fishing season. What kind of bait do I need?'" Ody laughed, and Gary Wohnt nodded approvingly. I felt empty as a pocket. I was not with my people.

"I have to pee." I rose and walked over to the public bathrooms, wondering if I could "accidentally" trip and break my itchy wrist corsage. My jean shorts and white T-shirt simply did not do it justice. Inside the bathroom stall, I dropped my bottoms and balanced over the toilet seat perched on top of a hole in the ground. The salty, pungent odor of outhouse and darkness closed in on me, and I held the carnations close to my nose to cover the smell.

I peed, listening to my tinkling echo in the pit. I dreamed of having to throw up so I could stay in the outhouse longer. Straight across from me, someone had scrawled, "I screwed your mother!" Down and to the left, someone else had written, "Go home dad. You're drunk!" I did a little more recreational reading before I stood.

I reluctantly walked around the interior cement divider to the wall mirror. It looked wavy and hand-pounded, like polished steel, and I couldn't see myself very well because the only light was coming through a square opening toward the ceiling. I squirted out some hand sanitizer from the dispenser and finally decided I couldn't hide out in there any longer. On my way out, I passed a large scrawl that read, "No matter how good she looks, some other guy is sick and tired of putting up with her crap." I crossed it out with a pen tied to the wall and wrote, "I think, therefore I am single." Not one of my wittier moments, but at least I had made a mark.

Actually, I had always wondered who had the energy to write on bathroom walls. Now I knew. It was people on bad dates. I steeled myself and stepped out into the lowering sun. Where I stood now, with Chief Wenonga and the terrible trio behind me, I could see the full brilliance of West Battle Lake. The sun was on the far side, sliding toward the water, and sailboats and fishing crafts glided across the lake. I could hear the faraway sounds of children swimming and splashing in the water, though I wasn't close enough to see them.

There was a light breeze keeping the buzzing mosquitoes to a minimum, and the temperature was still in the eighties but dropping. It would be a beautiful night. I was going to go back, eat my food, make polite small talk, and walk back to Gina's. This wasn't so bad. I could do this.

"Hey, Mira," Kennie called, waving her jangly-braceleted arm at me. "Y'all come over here and tell us if this looks infected to you!"

I shuffled over and dutifully examined the scabby scratch on Ody's knee. When I told him I thought salve and a Band-Aid would take care of it, he looked relieved and adjusted his glasses. "I had a partner who lost part of a leg to a scratch gone bad. Right below his knee. I swore that was never going to happen to me."

"It's good to have dreams, Ody." If there were such a thing as date indemnity, I would be considered uninsurable. Actually, my date with the transsexual professor had been one of my better encounters. On the other end of the scale was my night out with the regular from Perfume River, the Vietnamese restaurant I had worked at in the Cities. He was from China, studying neurology at the U of

M. We used to make small talk through his broken English and my lunch rushes.

One night he came in with a single yellow rose and laid it on the front counter with a note that said, "You go with me out?" I was so flattered by the attention that I agreed, despite his greasy hair and ill-fitting pants. For our date, we saw *Cyrano de Bergerac* at the college theater and ate burgers at Annie's in Dinkytown. I talked, and he smiled and nodded, his eyes never leaving my face.

I let him walk me back to my apartment, and at the end of the night, he kissed the palm of my hand. There was no sexual attraction, and our language differences put the kibosh on intellectual attraction, so I wrote it off as a nice night with a friend. He had different ideas. He started by having a dozen roses and a red and black negligee delivered to the restaurant. Apparently, "Do me" was not a common Chinese phrase expressing interest in another's delightful conversational ability, as I had thought on our date.

When I thanked him but explained I wasn't interested, he had size-seven brown suede calf boots sent to the restaurant, including a note asking for my social security number so he could always find me. The gifts grew more bizarre, until finally, on my day off, he stopped by the restaurant with an envelope stuffed with twenty-dollar bills. He told my coworker he would never bother me again because he was returning to his country, and would I please to buy myself something to heal my heart? I spent the money on books.

At least with Ody, I was pretty sure I knew what I was getting. The four of us sat down to a meal of smoked salmon (which looked raw and tasted like salty fish with lighter fluid poured over it), Easy Cheese, crackers, and Boone's Farm strawberry wine.

"It's not Boone's *Farm*, honey, it's *Boone's* Farm. It's all in how you say it," Kennie told me as she poured the sweet wine. For dessert, we ate Oreo cookies, which was so far the high point of the evening. Fortunately, no one talked as we ate. Once the cheese can was empty and the fish was just bones, the men sat back and began sucking leftovers out of their teeth.

Ody undid the top button of his Wrangler shorts to get a little more breathing room. "I caught that fish myself, Mira. I'm real good with fish."

Maybe the *Boone's* Farm was getting to me, but I swear that was some sort of lewd remark. "I don't like fishing, and I don't really like fish, to tell you the truth. They're too wet. I like dry food, like chips and bread."

This sparked some indignation in Ody, and he launched into a lecture about the benefits of eating God's creatures fresh from their habitat. I tuned him out and looked around for an escape. I saw it in the form of Jed limping slightly down the road past the park. He must have been on his way back to the Last Resort, and he had someone with him.

"Hey, Jed!" I waved him over desperately before I realized he was walking with Johnny Leeson. I pulled my hand back like it was holding a ripcord and clamped my mouth shut. Of course this would be the one time Jed was actually paying attention in his life. Belatedly, I remembered that the last time I had seen Jed was right after I stunned him and his bongo-playing compadre in the woods near Shangri-La.

He loped over, with Johnny following casually behind him. "Hey, Mira. You on a double date?" He was wearing a Def Leppard T-shirt over torn jeans, and he had a red bandana holding back his brown curls. Johnny wore a bright white T-shirt, which matched his smile and set off his nut-brown skin. The shirt hugged his broad shoulders and just skimmed the second snap of his button-fly Levi's, nicely showcasing his narrow hips. He smelled clean, like fresh laundry and newly cut grass.

I looked at Kennie, still in her Alvin and the Chipmunks get-up with her nesting-chipmunk hair, Gary Wohnt, who had pulled down his Erik Estrada cop sunglasses and was reapplying lip balm, and Ody, in his wife beater with his Wranglers undone and smelling of the fish he was still sucking out of his eyeteeth. "No, Jed, I was just visiting with these people."

Ody leaned over and brushed a piece of hair from my face. "No need to be modest, girl. I ain't ashamed to be with you."

I tried not to cry and turned back to Jed, ignoring the strange look Johnny was giving me. "What are you up to?"

"Johnny and I are running some errands for my mom. We figured it'd be a waste of a good night to drive. Hey, man, that show at Shangri-La was a kicker, no? When you disappeared and all that?" He nodded his head agreeably. Johnny had moved off and was studying Chief Wenonga, his shoulders in an angry set. Or was I imagining it? His profile was tanned and muscular, and his strong hands, the ones I often imagined twisted in my hair as he pulled me in for a passionate kiss, were fisted at his sides.

I turned my attention back to Jed, who did not seem bothered at all that I had made his hair extra curly that night. "Yeah, sorry about the stun gun. I was a little freaked out."

"What?" Jed asked.

"The shock I gave you when I jumped out of the bongo."

Jed's smile was confused but welcoming.

"You know, when I jumped out, zapped you, and you fell to the ground?"

Jed looked at Gary Wohnt and then back at me, winking conspiratorially. "Sure, you *zapped* me. I was real *zapped* that night."

Cripes. Jed didn't even know I had stun-gunned him. He thought it was just another high. "Okay, yeah. Zapped." I couldn't be heard over the now-frenzied tooth-sucking coming from the cop dates. I wanted to tap out "Help Me" in Morse code, but I didn't know how. I desperately wanted Johnny to know that I wasn't on a date, but the truth was, I was on a date, and I had no reason to think he cared. I felt miserable.

"Okay, then, we'll see ya around," Jed said. "Say, Chief Wohnt, when will we get back that dive suit that Mira found in Whiskey?"

"When we find out who planted the body."

"That makes sense, but it'd sure be nice to rent it out to someone else." Jed and Johnny took off, Johnny flashing me one last unreadable glance. I was left alone to make conversation in this wasteland. I examined my three options—Kennie, who was filing her nails, Ody, who was talking about the pros and cons of field dressing, and Gary Wohnt. "So, Chief, you still have the Last Resort dive suit that body was in?"

Silence.

"Did you confiscate the suits from the other divers who rented them from the Last Resort?"

The Chief shifted a toothpick from one side of his mouth to the other. I was a lot of work for him. "We investigated the people who rented them. They are all either staying at the Last Resort or at Glendalough, and they all came up clean. We did not take their dive suits."

"None of them were staying at Shangri-La?"

"None."

"Not even one rented to someone staying at Shangri-La?"

"None."

I shielded my eyes from the sun so I could watch Jed and Johnny walking away. Why had Jed lied to me about Jason Blunt, current Shangri-La resident extraordinaire, renting three dive suits from him? Then I remembered the water puddle under the dive suit I had borrowed from Jed, the dive suit he claimed hadn't been used in a long time. Maybe Jason hadn't rented his suits—maybe he had borrowed them just like me. Jed had mentioned that he had partied with Jason. Had he done more? Was he Jason's accomplice in all of this? Goofy, stoner Jed? I didn't want to believe it.

My stomach was roiling, and now it wasn't just because I had eaten canned cheese and questionable fish. "I don't feel so good. I think I need to go home."

Kennie looked indignant. "The night is young! I spent a lot more time working for you last night, and I didn't even get a free meal out of it."

Ody burped. "I'd walk you home, but these here legs are more ornamental than functional." He winked at me. Or he had something in his eye. "When will we be meeting again, little lady?"

I tried to be vague without being rude. "Oh, you'll know when we meet again." Because I'll be the one screaming and running the other way. "Thank you for the . . . food. And Kennie, I think we're even."

She scowled at me, but I would not be deterred. I needed self-respect and sleep. I saluted Chief Wenonga and hightailed it to Gina's couch.

FOURTEEN

WHEN I WOKE THE next morning, Gina was sitting at the foot of the sofa drinking coffee and waiting for me to open my eyes with all the patience of a child on Christmas morning. She had already walked, fed, and watered Luna and opened a can of Tender Vittles for Tiger Pop. All that was left to do was stare at me until I awoke.

As soon as I stirred, she pounced. "Why didn't you wake me up when you got home?"

"Because I figured if you were asleep by eight, you probably needed to stay asleep." I stretched and pulled the sheet back over me. I hated sleeping over at other people's houses. It wasn't comfortable.

"You were home by eight o'clock? No kissing?"

"No kissing. I did get to see the lower end of his belly button when he unsnapped his pants so he could eat more, though."

"You're shittin' me." She shook her head in disbelief. "I wipe other people's butts for a living, and that grosses me right out."

"Yeah. The best part came when Johnny Leeson met my date."

She set her coffee down and covered her mouth with both hands in a display of shock. "NO! Hot Johnny saw you on a date with a greasy old cop?"

"Ody was his name."

"Girl, you lost some points there."

"You think? I've slid down from 'dorky stalker lady who buys more seeds than she needs' to 'dorky stalker lady who buys more seeds than she needs, starring in the Appalachian Love Connection.'"

Gina laughed. "You're timing's not so good, either. Word on the street is Johnny just broke up with Liza. Last night would have been a good night to seem available."

I groaned and replayed the strange looks Johnny had given me last night. Had he been considering me as Liza's replacement? If he had, I'm sure the Ody glow on me had quickly done away with that idea. Who would want to date someone who dated an Ody? It'd be like wearing your grandma's clothes.

Gina studied my face and laughed kindly. "It's not that bad. Anyhow, I gotta go to work. What's on your plate for today?"

"I'm not sure yet. How well do you know Jed Heike?" I shared how he had lied to me about renting dive suits to Jason and how I had a bad feeling he was somehow hooked up in the planted dead body and wounded circus performer.

Gina screwed up her face in reflection "You know, I did hear that the Last Resort was going under. They don't get enough business. You think he'd hook up with Jason for the money?"

"I think he'd do anything to help out his parents."

Gina frowned. "But steal stolen jewelry? And arrange the shooting of a circus performer? You don't even know if one is related to the other. You gotta find that out before you incriminate anyone."

"I suppose, but that's a little too much coincidence for me. A person could go a whole lifetime without witnessing a little guy getting shot. To have that happen at the same time a fake dead body is planted in the lake near where hundreds of thousands of dollars of jewelry is likely hidden is out of the question."

"All I'm saying is you don't want to spend the energy worrying about what Jed has or hasn't done until you find out what is really going on."

"I suppose. Aren't you going to be late for work?" I pulled myself off the couch. I had to go to work, too. I wanted to get in early so I didn't miss Wicket W. Warrick's call.

"I don't work until ten today. The bathroom is all yours." Gina shuffled off into the kitchen and then turned back to me, a girlish smile on her face. "Say, Leif and I are going out on Friday. He said it's going to be a surprise, but I hope he takes me to the casino."

I mirrored her smile. "That's great, G. And you guys have set up counseling appointments?"

She looked at her feet. "We might. Right now we just want to try it the old-fashioned way."

Around here, and maybe everywhere in the world, the old-fashioned way meant he did what he wanted to do and she ignored it. It made me too sad to comment, so I just nodded and got ready for a grueling day of schlepping books. I cleaned myself up, gave Luna and Tiger Pop some attention, and was in the library by nine o'clock. I used the time before I opened up to take care of the duties I had been neglecting the last few days. I shelved books, dusted and vacuumed, watered plants, and even cleaned the windows. I rifled through the library mail, which was mainly glossy advertisements for new books, several overdue book fines getting paid, and a few random bills.

When Warrick called, I was basking in the afterglow of a vigorous cleaning, my face flushed and a relaxed smile on my face.

"Yeah, this the newspaper lady?" His voice was distinctly male, but high, like it was squeezed out.

"I am a reporter at the *Battle Lake Recall*. Are you the guy who was shot Monday night?"

I heard him puff up proudly on the other end of the line. "That I am. Nikolai Romanov is the name, and crowd-pleasing is my game."

"Romanov? I thought your name was Wicket W. Warrick." I grabbed a miniature pencil and a sheet of paper from the printer to take notes.

He chuckled condescendingly. "That's just one of my many stage names. I didn't know who I was talking to yesterday when I called. The nature of my work requires me to cultivate an air of mystery and fantasy."

"I'm sure. So the Romanov Traveling Theater troupe is yours?"

"It is."

"And you have a story to tell me?"

"I do. I will tell it to you on the south shore of Whiskey Lake at midnight tonight."

"What?" My voice came out a couple notes higher than normal. If you look in the dictionary under *dumb*, you would find "one who meets a carnival performer on the lam in a secluded area at midnight." I hedged. "How about we meet when it's light out?"

"How about I tell my story to the *Star Tribune*?"

How about I didn't give a shit about the competition. I did need to find out how Jason was caught up in all of this, though, or he would haunt me ad infinitum. I peeked in the purse I had started to carry and reassured myself that my trusty Z-Force was still nestled inside. "Fine. Give it to me in girl directions."

"You know where the public-access boat landing is on Whiskey?"

"Yup."

"Go to the boat landing. Face the water. Walk a hundred yards to your right. I'll be waiting. Be quiet, dress in black, bring a small tape recorder, and don't be late. And come alone, or I'll disappear like dust in the wind."

Good lord. What sort of self-respecting circus performer quoted Kansas? "Fine."

I hung up the phone and unlocked the door to let in the ten or so people who were lining up. I don't think the library had ever been this busy. The *Star Tribune* contest was bringing a lot of business to town. Most of them were magazine readers, which is the library equivalent of window shoppers, but a few signed up for library cards and mentioned that they were enjoying their stay.

Over lunch hour, I closed the library for a quick dash to the Fortune Café. Nancy was behind the counter in a green-checkered apron that read, "I'm Not Gay, But My Girlfriend Is." Small-minded people avoided Sid and Nancy and their café, which was great for the rest of us. Their sexuality served as a great social filter.

Actually, the biggest customer base for the Fortune was Sid and Nancy's church group. The two were very active at Nordland Lutheran and were always a favorite when it came time for bake sales and other events that involved desserts. I was still surprised they hadn't been stoned right out of town, which maybe made me the small-minded one.

Nancy waved me to the front of the line because she knew I was on my lunch break. "Hello, Mira! What're you in the mood for today?"

"Just a roasted garlic bagel and some green tea, Nance." I slid my travel mug over to her. "Thanks."

"Say, did Sid call you?"

I grabbed the tea and angled the bagel out of her hands—she knew I didn't want a bag—and gave her my money. "No. About what?"

"I'll let her tell you. She's in back loading the oven." Nancy jerked her head toward the back room, wiped her hands on her apron, and turned to the customer behind me.

I felt like a trespasser when I stepped into the kitchen. I had never been in this room before, and it smelled great. Big steel ovens lined the walls, with flour-covered tables full of rising bread filling the middle. Off to the side was a storage room with ingredients cleanly labeled, covered, and kept off the ground on a silver wire shelf. The only thing missing was Sid.

"Hello?"

"Hey, Mira!" Sid appeared from behind one of the stoves. She was smiling, but she looked harried. Flour dusted her hair, and her arms were loaded with trays of raw cookie-dough balls.

"Nancy said you wanted to talk to me?"

"Yeah, it's nothing really. It might just be a rumor. The divers that are staying at Glendalough? Well, they were in for coffee this morning, and they said they've scoured Whiskey Lake from top to bottom, north to south, and there's no necklace in a box there. They were going to go down one more time, and if they didn't find anything, they were going to lodge a complaint."

"So they think it was never sunk in the lake?"

"That, or someone has it and doesn't want anyone to know for some godforsaken reason. Just thought I'd let you know, since you're the reporter and all." She winked at me and loaded her cookie sheets into the oven.

"Thanks, Sid." I didn't know what to make of this new information. Certainly, diving is not an exact science. Visibility is often poor, and objects in lakes, especially spring-fed lakes, have a tendency to move. The people at the *Star Tribune* must have known this, and since they wanted the box found, if it was still there, it *was* surprising that no one had come across it yet. After all, it had been three days since the box had supposedly been hidden.

I pondered this as I walked to the *Recall* office. Ron was at the front counter when I strolled in, the phone still growing out of his ear. I waited impatiently, but he wasn't off by the time I had eaten my bagel and drunk most of my tea.

I pulled up a chair right next to him and stared at him, inches from his face, without blinking. He shooed me like a fly, but I didn't move. He finally sighed and stood up to rifle through a file cabinet, the phone cradled between his shoulder and ear.

He passed me the pink note onto which I had transcribed the code, and I grabbed it eagerly. I looked down at the scribblings, my tea and impatience forgotten. Ron had crossed out all the letters and written new letters over those, sometimes crossing out his guesses and writing on top of those. The letters were four high in some cases, but if I followed the hills, this is what the code I had stolen from the rum room really said:

With your back to the kissing tree walk seven steps northwest kneel 23 left 12 right 11 left.

There were question marks next to all three numbers, and he had circled the original numbers—76, 87, and 88—but that wasn't the beginning of my questions. What was a kissing tree? Was I supposed to kneel twenty-three times, or were there twenty-three of something left? Twenty-three left minus twelve that were right did leave eleven, but what did that mean? This was a puzzle within a puzzle.

I pulled the list of Shangri-La's stolen jewelry out of my purse. There were twenty-eight pieces of jewelry recorded missing, not including "assorted diamond earrings." That didn't seem to be what the code numbers were referring to. The numbers almost sounded like a dance—kneel, go twenty-three steps to the left, twelve to the right, and eleven to the left. That felt a little overdone, but not surprising from a woman who would write a secret code in the first place. Once I figured out what the kissing tree was, I hoped this would be a lot clearer.

I dashed back to the library and searched through the Otter Tail County reference books. No mention of a kissing tree. I went online to do a search of the same, and I came up with obscure references to musical bands and some strange religion, and even a funny website where a woman had created a virtual tree consisting of pictures of people who had kissed her—but no landmarks in this area.

On a whim, I called over to the Senior Sunset and asked for Mrs. Berns. If there was anyone in this town who would know where people went to kiss in the 1920s, it was Mrs. Berns.

"Yello."

"Mrs. Berns?"

"Last time I checked."

"This is Mira from over at the library. Say, do you know if there is a kissing tree in Battle Lake?"

"Oh honey, who told you you have to be under a tree to kiss? That's malarkey. You kiss anywhere you feel like kissing!"

I could sense her getting steamed up on the other end. "Thank you, Mrs. Berns. I'll take that to heart. But I'm writing an article on the history of love in Battle Lake, and I want to know if there was some place you all went to make out back in the day, say in the twenties or thirties?"

"Ooooh, that was a long time ago, honey. Most of the twenties are just a drunken blur for me, anyhow. Hold on while I go ask around."

Twelve minutes later, she was back on the phone, cackling.

"You still here?"

"Yup." I had been paging through *Us* magazine, reading a strangely compelling article about Paris Hilton, the Zsa Zsa Gabor of the new millennium, while she was away. I knew Mrs. Berns would remember me eventually, and I needed to catch up on what the stars ate during their photo shoots anyhow.

"I plumb forgot we were talking on the phone." I heard some more chittering in the background. "The good news is, I found out about your kissing tree. You know where Chief Wenonga sits?"

Boy, did I. And I knew where I wished he'd sit, too: right in my front yard so I could wake up to him every morning. "Yes ma'am."

"Well, straight across the road from him, there's a little dip as you go down toward the lake. There's a grove of trees in that dip, and I guess all the kids used to sneak there to make out, long before the Chief was around."

I knew the grove of trees, and it was about twenty-three strides from the Chief. That might account for that number, only the Chief was built fifty years after Regina would have hidden the jewels. The only thing for it was to check out the area after I closed the library.

FIFTEEN

THE AFTERNOON DRAGGED ON like yet another war documentary on the History Channel, but closing time finally came. Normally, I would let people finish what they were doing before I closed up, but that afternoon I physically herded people out of the library. Leylanda tried to drag herself and Peyton in for some last-minute reading, but I would have none of it.

"We just need one book. I know exactly where it is."

"Leylanda, it's five after. It's closing time. Come back tomorrow."

Peyton grabbed my hand. "If you don't let me get some new books, I'll have to learn how to make carob almond-butter cookies tonight."

I sighed. "Okay, sweetie. You go grab what you want, and your mom and I will wait for you here. You don't even have to check it out." I wasn't letting Leylanda in. I knew she would make herself at home just to annoy me.

Leylanda glared at me, crossed her arms, set her shoulders, and waited. The silence must have been too much for her, because she started to make small talk against her will. "I saw you talking with Jason Blunt yesterday near the turtle races."

"Sure. Talking."

"He is quite a man."

"If by that you mean he's an abusive asshole, then I agree completely." I watched Peyton grab three of the most colorful new arrivals across the room. "How do you know Jason, anyhow? He doesn't seem like your type."

Leylanda sniffed. "We went to high school together. As to my type, you probably don't understand the nature of testosterone. You see, I am an alpha female, and I need an alpha male to equal out my power and drive for dominance." She set her shoulders and revealed this with the forced air of someone who has been through a lot of therapy.

I gave her my full attention. She was in the early stage of making a terrible but common error—mistaking one-way attention for a two-way attraction. I was no fan of hers, but she was another human being, and I cared about Peyton. "Leylanda, you've got a great daughter, and I'm sure you also have some good qualities of your own. Just relax a little, and don't be sucked in by Jason's nice-guy front. He's an insecure, violent creep, and he wears fur and eats genetically modified foods. And he doesn't recycle."

She sucked in her breath and covered her mouth with her small, birdlike hand, her eyes wide. "Come on, Peyton! Mommy says it's time to go! Come on now, Peyton."

Peyton handed me the books she had chosen as her mom dragged her past, and I grabbed them and fed them to her behind the alarm sensors so she wouldn't trigger the book-recovery system. She was almost through the door when she pulled free from her mom's grasp long enough to run back and hand me a stack of paper she had been crumpling in her seven-year-old fist. I unfolded them enough to see that they were crayon drawings. She was at a stage in her art career where she favored pastels. The first picture was of a house with a round yellow sun overhead, and she had scrawled her name on the bottom in tilting green. The second picture was of an animal, but I don't think anyone short of Dr. Moreau could have identified it. The third picture looked like a drawing of a family sitting around a dinner table, and at the bottom of that she had scratched out the words "math lab." That must be what Leylanda called homework time.

I left the pictures on the counter and locked the library door behind me. I took off toward Chief Wenonga at a jog and ran right into Johnny Leeson as I turned the side of the library, knocking both of us on our bumpers.

I was up first, dancing around like a fighter before a match. "Sorry, Johnny! I didn't see you!" I held out my hand. He grabbed it and pulled himself up. I suddenly was self-conscious of the June-bug-shaped lump on my noggin and tried to find a reason to hold my hand over my forehead while I talked. "You okay?"

"Yeah, I'm fine." He brushed dirt off his jeans, and I saw a raw spot on the palm of his hand.

"Shoot, I'm sorry. Look. You scraped your hand."

He glanced at it and rubbed it on his pants to get the gravel out. "It's not a big deal, Mira. It's just a scrape. I'll be fine." He did an unconscious head toss that moved his gold-flecked, shaggy hair out of his eyes for a second.

"Nice night, huh?"

He looked around, weighing the accuracy of my comment. "It is a nice night. How're your tomatoes holding up? Is the dill keeping the bugs away?"

"It is, but I think I'm overwatering. The color on the tomatoes isn't so good." My hand was over my lump, and I drummed the side of my head with my fingers in what I hoped was a nonchalant gesture.

He nodded his head, a reluctant smile teasing the corners of his mouth. "That can happen. We have some new automatic tomato waterers at the nursery so you don't have that problem. Stop by and I'll show 'em to you."

"That would be great!" I was smiling right up until the finch flew into the side of my head, above my right ear, and dropped to the pavement, stunned. I shrieked and jumped back a step. It shook its feathery little head, pooped, and took off again.

Johnny reached his strong brown hands out to me. "Are you okay? That had to hurt."

I was already hustling in the other direction, away from Johnny so he couldn't see the involuntary water filling my eyes. The birds were finally organizing their attack against me, and I wasn't going to let Johnny observe me going down. He had already seen me out with Ody, and I'm sure he had just seen the green and yellow bump pushing out of my head like a horn—how much embarrassment must I endure in front of him? I hollered at him over my shoulder, ignoring his bemused expression. "Oh no, didn't hurt at all. I do that all the time at home!"

It took me about ten minutes to reach Halverson Park and Chief Wenonga's statue, and I didn't see any bird gangs flashing their blades on the way, so I calmed down some, though I had the

mother of all headaches. I decided the finch had been a lone gun-
man, trying to protect Johnny from me, the un–Snow White.

I found the grove of kissing trees straight across the road, just
like Mrs. Berns had said. They were an unassuming cluster of pop-
lars with the road directly behind them, the lake straight in front of
and to one side of them, and Sandy Beach Resort to the other side.
Peonies blooming everywhere scented the air like delicious white
trash roses. With my back to the trees, I paced seven steps with the
sun's downward trajectory off to my left. Then I walked twenty-
three steps to the right, toward Sandy Beach, which led me straight
into the volleyball pit. Twelve steps in any direction still left me in
the pit. Anything hidden here would have been unearthed when
this resort was built, so unless Regina had hidden the loot in West
Battle Lake, I was at the wrong spot.

My shoulders slumped, and I kicked at the sand of the court.
There was nothing to do but head back to my car in the library
parking lot. Finding the jewelry before Jason had been my trump
card, and this search was a dead end. My only hope now was that
Nikolai Romanov would tell me something incriminating about
Jason tonight.

I heard the siren before I saw the lights, though it all shrieked
past me in under three seconds. Police racing through Battle Lake
were a rarity, and I had a thick, bad feeling about this. The blue
and red screeched left on Oak Avenue, about seven blocks up from
where I was, and I took off jogging. Gardening, swimming, and
walking with Luna kept me in pretty good shape, but as a grown-
up, I hadn't found much call to run, and my body didn't know what
to do with itself. I puffed about four blocks before I was forced to
slow to a brisk walk.

Oak Avenue abuts the woods, mostly maple and oak, so the majority of the houses were very nice and situated on wooded lots. The one exception was the freakish white box of a house where Leylanda and Peyton lived. It was as tucked into the woods as a house in town could be. Chief Wohnt's car was parked in their driveway, his lights off but his door open. I slowed to a walk, and in fact considered turning around. I had just seen them only a half hour ago, and I could picture them tucked in the safety of their living room, reading the books Peyton had picked out, eating roasted soy nuts, and chugging organic ginger ale. I didn't want to disturb that picture, because I knew in my aching heart how quickly bad things happened to good people.

I forced my feet to move through the ominous quicksand of my fears and lumbered into their yard. The front door was flung open, and inside I could see Leylanda on the couch, her neighbor propping her up as her body heaved in sobs.

Leylanda's voice quivered. "She wanted to read in her room alone. She wasn't out of my sight for more than ten minutes. I swear! She's been kidnapped!" Her eyes stared blankly as she cried, and two rivers of snot ran out of her nose.

Peyton was missing. My stomach clenched, and I felt the unbearable, aching fog of loss that I hadn't experienced as acutely since my dad died. I knew what it was like to be a girl alone in the world, and Peyton was too young to experience that depth of fear and loneliness.

The neighbors who had gathered looked up at me as I entered, but no one stopped me. I tried to ask Gary Wohnt for details, but I felt like I was floating above the room, watching the actors stage their play.

Chief Wohnt spoke into his shoulder radio, and I heard some feedback, but it crackled too much for me to make sense of it. He next spoke to the inconsolable Leylanda. "I need to know everyone you've talked to and everywhere you've been in the last twenty-four hours."

Leylanda struggled to pull herself together, but it was beyond her. "Somebody took my daughter! She needs to sleep in her own bed or she's up all night! Who will practice Spanish with her if I'm not there?"

"You need to calm yourself down," Wohnt urged, not unkindly. "She likely just ran away and is in the vicinity."

Leylanda's crazy eyes focused for the first time, and they shot zingers at Wohnt. "And I suppose she took the whole window frame out by herself and set it on the ground outside her bedroom before she ran off?"

I backed out of the house, remembering the time I had run away from home. I was nine, and my dad and mom were fighting about him getting a job. My mom said he needed to get out of the house and be with people, and he said that me and mom were already too many people for him, and if he had it his way, he would have lived alone. I decided to make his wish come true. I packed a bag of oyster crackers, a blanket, and my favorite Judy Blume book and spent the night in the cornfield. I was cold, and alone, and scared that when I got home no one would be there. The sad truth is that to a child, any home is better than no home.

And right now, Peyton was without her home in the hands of who-knows-what. I started pacing in ever-widening circles around her house, calling her name as if she were a lost pet. In the back of my mind, I noticed that the neighborhood was organizing, and soon, most of the town of Battle Lake would be looking for tiny Peyton McCormick.

SIXTEEN

WHEN I WAS GROWING up in safe, acceptably abnormal Paynesville, there were two things that really got me keyed up. One was when it was my turn to have Connie Christopherson solve my Rubik's Cube. She was the only person in all of fifth grade who had figured it out, and she hadn't even read the book. For a small donation of Pixy Stix, she would click-clack-click your cube until each side was a paean to monochromaticity.

It was beautiful—art and organization united—and it never lasted more than one class period. It took that long for me to convince myself that if she could do it, I could too. I only messed it a little bit at a time, starting by moving the middle square of color on all six sides. I felt confident that if I started slowly, I could find my way back. This delusion assured continuing business for Connie and kept her in Pixy Stix well into sixth grade, when the handheld Simon game and Garbage Pail Kids cards hit Paynesville via Penny Johnson's visiting cousin from Texas and effectively erased Rubik's Cube, Snake, and Triangle from our consciousness.

The other thing that excited me was when I was allowed computer lab time and could play Oregon Trail for a full hour. The middle school owned only four computers at the time, all Apple IIe's, and to get access to them, you had to be part of the gifted program. The first skill we learned on the Apples was basic line programming, which involved creating a program that looked like a ball bouncing down colored stairs on the screen.

I rushed to accomplish this so I could begin playing Oregon Trail, a control-loving girl's ticket to joy. In the game, you started out as your average pioneer about to embark on a new life in the faraway state of Oregon. The trick was, you needed to decide what to take with you to survive the journey—you only had a certain amount of space allotted in the covered wagon and a certain amount of money to buy food, bullets, and supplies with.

Your quest was played out on a map-like screen charting the wagon's progress in relation to famous towns and landmarks such as Big Hill and the Shawnakee Trading Post. About ten real-life seconds after you hit the Trail, one of the following would happen: (1) You would run into a buffalo stampede that you could opt to hunt, and hunting stampeding buffalo is like shooting fish in a barrel. Literally. The bullets moved in aching slowness across the green screen. (2) You would spot a group of strangers and choose how to react. "Approaching" them leads to a fight, as does "circle wagons." In either case, you needed to have your guns ready.

The game was designed to build real-life decision-making and problem-solving skills by making a kid the leader of a wagon party. Although I may never have directly applied these skills, I derived infinite pleasure out of controlling my own destiny, if even only for an hour. I particularly missed that experience as, just before midnight, I began my walk to the public access to meet a dwarf on the run from the law and pondered the whereabouts of a scared seven-year-old who may never know the pleasures of pre-teen fads and dim-witted computer games. I had spent four hours scouring the woods by her house for any trace of her, and soon, the entire town was searching. Now that it was dark, hundreds of flashlights stabbed the air in and around Battle Lake like fireflies.

Walking carefully through the dark toward my meeting, I swear I heard an audible click when I mentally separated myself from Peyton's situation. I could feel my heart turning a little colder and my mind a little harder. If I kept worrying about her and imagining what she was enduring right now, I would go crazy. I had learned how to separate myself from emotions and circular thoughts when my dad killed himself and two others in that horrible car accident, and I would use those skills now. Plenty of others were searching for her, and there was nothing more I could do for her tonight.

I knew from Sunday's post-fake-body trek that it would take me under forty-five minutes to hike to the south-side Whiskey Lake access, and since Nikolai demanded utter stealth, I figured walking would make me quiet as a ghost. I might even be able to sneak up on him and give myself the upper hand, if only for a couple moments.

I decided to stick to the woods and prairie, which would keep me on Sunny's property right up until the access. That way I wouldn't need to answer questions if someone passed me on the road at midnight. The slice of moon in the brilliant June sky didn't provide as much light as the twinkling stars, but between the two, I was able to find my way just fine.

The mosquitoes were tolerable, and swooping bats feasted off the ones I didn't smush. For some reason, bats didn't bother me like birds did. Maybe it was because they were up front about their personalities. They were leathery flying mice not trying to be anything else. Plus, anything that ate mosquitoes in Minnesota had a certain sense of holiness about it.

A rabbit darting from behind a rock and into a hole startled me, but otherwise, the landscape was serene and space-like in its starlit stillness. The only sounds were my shoes gathering dew, the far-off resonance of cars cruising Highway 210 a couple miles off, and cows lowing. The air smelled charged with water, and I wondered if a storm was on the way.

When I reached the top of the sumac-speckled hill that over-looked both the public access and Shangri-La Island, I crouched down and clicked the illuminating button on my watch. It was 11:37. I was early. Shangri-La was down for the night. Not even birds moved on the island.

The access, about two hundred yards away from where I was hunkered down, was a different story. I spotted a small figure wobbling through the woods. He or she looked like a child from here, but I assumed it was Nikolai. I squinted but couldn't make out any more details except that the person looked alone.

Feeling slightly more confident, I stayed low to the ground and crept toward the access. I caught my breath behind a thick oak tree and tugged my stun gun out of the plastic-lined neck pouch I had put it and the miniature tape recorder in to keep them dry and my hands free. I strapped the Z-Force to the belt of my stealth outfit—black turtleneck, black jeans with a black belt, hair pulled back in a black ponytail holder, and black tennis shoes left over from my waitressing days. I steeled myself and walked quietly and confidently across the open expanse of the boat launch and into the edge of the woods on the other side. I counted off a hundred yards as I stepped silently into the treed border and was only mildly frightened when a hand grabbed at me.

"About time you showed up!" a voice hissed. Nikolai's round white face glowered at me in the darkness.

"I'm early." I studied Nikolai. In the moonlit dark, his hair was a nondescript brown, and I guessed his eyes were also. He had a large head and puffed as he talked. The top of his cranium came to my boob level, which would make him a little shy of four feet. He was dressed in all black, too, and seemed injury-free and in perfect health save for the shortness of breath. This was interesting, since the last time I had seen him, he appeared to be suffering from a fatal gunshot wound on Shangri-La Island.

"If I've been waiting, you're not early. Did you bring the tape recorder?"

I patted the neck pouch. "Right here."

He acted peeved, but he wasn't going to let that derail his fifteen minutes of fame. Hands on hips, he glared at me while he spoke in a tremulous voice underscoring his words. "Turn it on and settle back for the tale of a lifetime. It will amaze, thrill, and chill you. It will give you anticipation, perspiration, and exultation. You will feel delighted, excited, and ignited. When I tell you the tale of the Romanov Traveling Theater troupe, you will sigh, cry, and not want to say goodbye . . ."

This is how the talk went for over a half an hour, judging by the location of the moon. Nikolai told me how he founded the theater troupe when he failed out of clown school, how he recruited other disenfranchised clowns and circus acts into his troupe, what amazing acting abilities they had cultivated, how they branched out into a carnival show to attract children, and so on.

I was just about to interrupt him when he said something that made me sit up like a dahlia in the August sun: ". . . is when I met a fellow artist like myself with really good weed. He works over at the Last Resort, and we recruited him to play bongos at the Shangri-La show."

"Is this fellow artist tall and lanky with curly brown hair, and does he talk like Shaggy from Scooby Doo?"

"Yes, he does, though that is simply one of the many faces he wears." Nikolai stretched and brought his voice back to a less theatrical level. "That cat has a lot of fantastic ideas. He did agree that staging my own death would be a coup de theatre."

Jed. He *was* involved in this. My stomach bravely fought an onslaught of acid, and then surrendered to my stress in a pitiful gurgle. Was Jed just another man hiding a sinister side? "That was quite the performance. So you staged your death on Shangri-La Island to get attention?"

"For the craft, madam, for the craft," he said impatiently. "And for a little extra cash. But you are missing the point. I had my audience spellbound. It was the greatest possible moment in live theater."

"Wait. Someone paid you to stage your death? Who and why?"

Nikolai grinned like the Cheshire cat and rubbed his hands together. "Let's just say that someone had a criminal record and wanted to draw a little heat away. A harmless goal, really, but it made for spectacular theater, and now every officer in the county is looking for yours truly. I'm sure I would have thought of the plan on my own if he hadn't presented the idea to me."

I was mentally racing through past conversations with Jed, trying to remember if he had ever mentioned a criminal record. He might be goofy enough to talk Nikolai into staging his own death for the heck of it, but I don't think he was creative or motivated enough to come up with the plan. "If *who* hadn't presented the idea to you?" I demanded.

Nikolai was clearly exasperated that I was focusing on what he saw as a minor detail. He drew himself up to his full four feet. "Did Houdini tell his audience how he unlocked his chains while buried alive? Does David Copperfield reveal where his disappearing tigers go?"

Jesus, for rhetorical questions. I needed to come at this a different way, because once I knew who had put Nikolai up to staging his own death, I would have a better idea if Jason was my biggest problem, if he had accomplices, or if there was someone else up to no good who I didn't even know about. I put the Jed issue onto the back burner for the moment and concentrated on distracting Nikolai into telling me who the person with the record was. "How'd you fool the paramedics into thinking you had been shot?"

He smiled arrogantly. "A stroke of genius."

According to Nikolai's story, the troupe's lizard-eyed emcee had a prescription for Guanabenz, a medication used to treat high blood pressure. Some research revealed that a little more than the prescribed dose would slow the user's heartbeat, contract his pupils, and put him in a semi-comatose state. Nikolai took the Guanabenz and had the emcee shoot him with blanks, then squished some fake blood pellets over his heart. Once the paramedics established he was stable but in serious condition, they applied pressure to stop his blood flow and took off.

"When we got to the hospital, I jumped off the gurney in the emergency room, did my trademark tap dance to the absolute astonishment of the medical staff, and was out the door, where the ringmaster was waiting in our tour van. It was beautifully executed at every point, and people will be talking about it for decades." Nikolai polished his fists on his shirt and beamed.

I wouldn't call that plan genius. It sounded like a string of dumb-and-luck beads to me. "You know, it's illegal to use emergency services as props."

"Hence, you and I meeting at midnight and the Romanov Traveling Theater troupe quietly disbanded and out of state for an unspecified period of time."

"Do you know anything about the little girl who is missing?"

Nikolai looked genuinely surprised and wounded. "No. I am an artist, not a criminal, and I don't hurt children."

"So you got me out here so I could write the story of your fabulous death and escape?" What I really wanted to know is why I was so close to so much staged death. It wasn't very funny.

"That's part of it. The important part." His voice and body seemed to shrink as he stepped outside of his theater guise and became a normal man weaseling for something. "The other part is I want you to get the box with the fake diamond planted in it for me. We can split the prize money seventy-thirty."

I snorted involuntarily. I hadn't seen that one coming. "Buddy, if I knew where the box was, I'd have found it by now, and I wouldn't give you any."

"That's why you need me. I know where the box is. The troupe and I were staying at a patron's acreage on the north side of this lake, and I watched three people in black dive suits slip into the creek that leads into the quiet side of the lake very early Monday morning. They had a black box tied to a rock and dragged it into the lake with them. I would have missed them except that I was up early planning my magnificent death and escape."

"Why didn't you have someone from your troupe get it?"

"None of us know how to dive."

"How do you know I know how to dive?"

Nikolai grunted. "Everyone knows that, m'dear. You're the one who got tangled up on that 'dead' body in front of Shangri-La."

"Humph." On principle, I didn't want to help him out, but there was a nice chunk of cash at stake. "Fifty-fifty."

"Sixty-forty."

"Fifty-fifty."

"Fifty-five-forty-five."

"Fifty-fifty. And you better take it, because I know where the creek is and I can just find the box all on my own now."

"Okay, fifty-fifty. But you can't find the box on your own without a little bit more information. Swear to me you will not take more than half the reward money for that box."

I held out my hand. "I swear."

"Okay, then, and that's on tape." He shook my hand with his child-sized free one and pointed at the recorder clipped to my waist, its tiny wheels spinning robotically in the starlight. "The reason no one has found the box yet is the divers wrapped it in a camouflage net. Their bubbles stopped about seventy-five yards straight out from the creek, so go due south from there and look for the netting on the bottom of the lake. Underneath that is our ticket to five thousand dollars."

A movement up the shore caught my eye. "Unless someone else finds it first." I pointed about two hundred yards east of us, where I saw one diver dragging another into the lake.

Nikolai chuckled softly. "Right on time. This one's on me."

I looked at him, amazed. I had written him off as a pompous actor midway through the interview, but he still had some secrets up his sleeve. I returned my attention to the two divers, and it took me a full minute before I realized what I was seeing. Someone was planting another body in the lake, and I didn't know if this one was real or not.

SEVENTEEN

From my perch on the edge of the woods, I couldn't make out the details of the tableau two hundred yards up the shore, except that the standing diver wore a dark dive suit with writing on the rump and had on a yellow tank. He had his facemask on and his regulator in and was breathing and splashing loudly. With the oxygen on his back and the body in his arms, he was moving with all the grace of a *Land of the Lost* Sleestack.

When he took his first full step, I saw he had a noticeable limp. Jed. The suited body he was hauling was tied to a rock, and I realized it had to be another bogus body or a very light one, because no normal human could drag a full-suited person and a rock while fully outfitted to dive. I had a shrieking notion that Jed may have Peyton strapped to his back, but I ignored it. I actively refused to believe Jed was evil. He was planting *fake* bodies, and I thought I knew why.

I was still hoping for more information from Nikolai, though he was proving to be craftier than I had given him credit for. "Who is it?" I whispered under my breath.

"You'll have to get the combination for that safe on your own, m'dear. I'm done for the night. I'll meet you back here tomorrow to get my half of the reward. Same time, same rules."

Nikolai took off into the woods, but I wasn't paying attention to him. I wasn't thinking about who had convinced him to pretend to die. I wasn't looking at the bubbles that now marked the ghoulish diver's underwater mission. I wasn't even thinking about Peyton. I was having a real, honest-to-goodness, light-bulb-sparking-over-my-head epiphany. Nikolai had said that I'd need to discover the combination for that safe on my own. It had been an offhand choice of words, but it had more meaning for me. Of course. Regina's code numbers were the combination to a safe: 23 left, 12 right, 11 left. Cosmic duh! I just had to find out what she meant by the kissing tree, and I'd have the jewels.

Unfortunately, I still had no charges to press against Jason. I would just have to settle for finding the jewels first—and an old-fashioned nose-thumbing in Jason's general direction. Still, I couldn't help considering what I had been dreading: that Jason was responsible for Peyton's disappearance. Was I just becoming paranoid, attributing all the bad things in town to him because he had attacked me a few years ago? I couldn't cloud my objectivity with a personal vendetta even though I had seen Jason with Peyton and Leylanda only the day before. What would a man in search of jewels want with a little girl?

Maybe the person with the criminal record who convinced Nikolai to shoot himself was a stranger, and maybe he had kidnapped Peyton for some unknown reason. Jason could simply be after the jewels in an aggressive fashion—not out of character for him. I needed more information. It seemed like my best bet was to speak with Leylanda tomorrow and find out if she knew more than she thought she did.

I mulled over hurrying back to my house now and calling the police to tell them someone was planting another body in the lake, but I had a heavy feeling that Jed wouldn't get treated well by law enforcement. I told myself I wasn't even 100 percent positive it was Jed. There could be more than one person in Otter Tail County with a limp. Anyways, I didn't want to pull any person power away from the search for Peyton.

And if it was Jed, I wanted to hear his side of the story before I turned him in. There would be no confronting ghost divers tonight. I quietly hiked the forty-five minutes back to my house, waved wistfully at my bed through the window, and drove to town to crash on Gina's couch.

I slept poorly, nightmares of Peyton on a fiery roller-coaster ride pockmarking the few hours of sleep I scratched out. I woke on Gina's couch near dawn, tired and crabby, Tiger Pop curled up on my feet and Luna snuffling at my ear. I took patient Luna for a long walk, noticing that the town was already wallpapered with posters of the missing seven-year-old and that either the searchers were up early or they had never gone to bed. The Channel 5 News crew was in front of the bank, interviewing an employee of Wood-lawn Resort. I heard her say she was one of the coordinators of the local search party and that they weren't going to stop looking until they found our girl. The camera lights glinted off the "Find Peyton" button on her chest, and she looked straight into the camera when she spoke. Small towns have big hearts for their children.

I snuffed the guilt bubble growing in me. I shouldn't have slept at all last night. I should have hunted for Peyton. No. I couldn't get this involved again. My dad had taught me the dangers of getting attached to another person. Besides, what could I do that the whole town wasn't already doing? My time was best spent getting my hands on those jewels and nailing Jason. I brought Luna back to Gina's and returned to the library just in time to open it at ten o'clock. Mrs. Berns was waiting outside and wearing a fuchsia running suit, which was ironic, since the only exercise she got didn't require clothes.

"You look like warm barf. You sleepin' okay?"

I turned the key to the front door and heard the tumbler click. Peyton's face was staring sweetly back at me from the flyer placed on the door. "Matter of fact, I'm not, Mrs. Berns. My life has been a little hectic lately." I was thinking that in addition to my worries for Peyton, my race to find the jewels, my investigative reporting, and my full-time library job, I also had two dear animals, a large lawn, and flower and vegetable gardens that I was neglecting. My life was running away without me.

"You should let some of your responsibility go, and I can help, dear. Here's my resumé. I'm your new part-time librarian."

I looked at the handwritten sheet of lined notebook paper she had shoved into my hand, the confetti edges still hanging on where she had ripped it out of a spiral tablet. In the center of the page, she had scribbled, "My name is Mrs. Berns, and I'm your new assistant librarian." Very concise.

"Mrs. Berns, I don't know if we have the budget for another librarian."

She cocked her head and waggled her finger at me. "You had enough money for you and Lartel, that wacko, swishy-pant-wearin' freak, so you got enough money for you and me. You tell me if you got someone better beggin' for this job."

She did have a point in that the line of people who wanted to sit in a stone building on a beautiful Minnesota summer day for minimum wage was only slightly longer than the line of Otter Tail County men who wanted to go into counseling to improve their personal relationships. "Okay, Mrs. Berns. I'll hire you on a trial basis. If you work out, I'll set you up for regular hours."

She clapped her hands and then rubbed them together. "You're a smart girl. The first thing we're going to do is get an adult section in here. All these namby-pamby books are a good front, but we know what people really want to read. And in back, you need a smoking room to draw the bar crowd. And this carpeting—"

"No! No changes! If you're going to work here, you have to remember that I'm the boss. This is the public library, not a pleasure palace. Now, why don't you start by shelving those books in the drop-off bin?"

I pointed at the box by the door, and she scowled at me, arms crossed on her chest, and then backed down. I sensed that this was the calm before the storm, and she was just gathering strength for a later confrontation. Until then, I was going to enjoy the help.

Mrs. Berns turned out to be an astonishingly efficient coworker when she wasn't reading over patrons' shoulders or goosing the male clientele. With her help, the library was looking tidy and more organized than it had since I started in March. It was an hour before closing, and there was nothing left to do.

"Why don't you go home, dear," she suggested. "You can get a little sleep or whatnot. I'll get these people out of here at closing and lock up."

The offer was tempting. Mrs. Berns had already worked alone at the library once and had not burned it down or gotten the chairs sticky in any after-hours orgy. Besides, I was itching to talk to Jed, and I also needed to walk Luna and then run home and mow my lawn before it became a wood tick sanctuary. That would give me time to talk to Leylanda tonight to see if I could make any connections between Peyton's disappearance and the other strangeness in town.

I just didn't know about leaving Mrs. Berns with the keys. She had a history of raucous and racy behavior. "I only have the one key, Mrs. Berns, and the city council gave me strict instructions not to lend it out when they gave me the job."

Mrs. Berns dug around in her white plastic purse, which was lying on the counter, and came out with a rapper-sized key ring. She methodically clinked through the metal passports. "Municipal liquor store, high school, cop shop . . . here it is! The Battle Lake Public Library. Looks like we're set."

I was astounded. "How'd you get keys to all those places?"

Mrs. Berns winked at me. "A woman's wiles. Plus, it's sort of a hobby of mine."

The realization that Mrs. Berns had probably already spent a lot of time alone in the library was oddly liberating. "It's a deal. Close it up at the top of the hour, and I'll meet you back here tomorrow morning at opening so we can draw up your schedule."

"It's a deal, homey." Mrs. Berns grabbed my hand in some sort of gangsta handshake and headed back to the stacks. I snatched my purse from behind the counter. It contained the tape and tape recorder I had used last night, and I wanted to listen to it again to see if I had missed any clues.

A short car drive brought me to West Battle Lake and the Last Resort. I took in the rundown look of the place, noticing for the first time that one of the cabin's roofs was sagging and that the boats tied to the dock were pretty banged up. Sal directed me to the hammock tied between two trees on the beach, where I found Jed snoozing, wearing nothing but bright aqua Bermuda shorts. He had a fresh bandage wrapped around his knee. I prodded him gently.

He snorted, stretched, and opened one eye. "Whaddya know for sure?" His wide smile was sincere.

"Not much these days, Jed. Your knee looks a little rough. How'd you say you hurt it again?"

He pushed himself to a seated position and rubbed the swollen area around the bandage. "I scraped it on a rock, diving."

"On Sunday, you said you twisted it unloading a boat and that you hadn't been diving in a while."

He looked at me once, quickly, and his cheeks flushed in embarrassment. "Yeah, I musta forgot. You know, it'd be great to find that box."

"It sure would be nice to have some extra money to fix up this place, wouldn't it?" I asked. "Business has been kinda slow here, according to Sal."

Jed nodded solemnly, and then his face brightened. "But it's already getting better, Mira! What with that fake dead body in front of Shangri-La, and then the shooting, no one wants to stay there anymore. We're full up for the first time in three summers."

I shook my head sadly. Jed was pretty transparent. "Jed, I know you planted that body that I found in Whiskey and another one last night. I saw you."

Jed's eyes grew big like fried eggs, and I could see the wheels turning behind them as he struggled to find a way out of this. Unfortunately, all the pot had rusted his cogs. A big, shiny tear formed at the corner of each eye. "Mira, I feel so shitty about that. I really do, man, and I know my karma is going to be sub-groovy. But I had to help my parents. I had to! I suppose you're gonna turn me into the Man?"

"What do you know about Jason Blunt?"

"Nothin', except he was a supreme toker back in high school. That man would do any drug you passed him. A little bit of a temper, but otherwise fun." Jed smiled happily at the memory.

"Is he involved in any of this?"

Jed looked puzzled. "Planting those two bodies to scare people off Whiskey Lake was my own idea, Mira. Nobody else even knows I did this."

Except for me and Nikolai. Jed wouldn't be earning the adjective "stealthy" anytime soon. "Why'd you tell me that Jason rented some dive suits from you?"

"It was the only name I could think of when you asked me. How'd you figure out it was me underwater surfin' the bodies?"

"Mostly dumb luck, Jed. I'll make a deal with you. You stop selling pot, stop planting bodies, and stop hanging out with actors and carnival folk, and I won't tell on you."

"Can I still smoke pot?"

"Until your head starts on fire."

"Deal!" He shook my hand enthusiastically and was wiggling like a puppy. He had been harboring guilt about his dead-body missions, and I had absolved him.

"I gotta go mow my lawn now. You stay out of trouble."

He tried to pull himself out of the hammock but winced when he attempted to bend his bad leg. "I can mow your lawn, Mira. I do all our grass here."

I'll bet. "That's okay, Jed. I need the downtime to think through some things. You get that cut looked at, all right?"

"My mom's taking me to the doctor this afternoon."

"Good. Oh, one more thing. You don't have a criminal record, do you?"

"Not me, but I do think I'm being watched. I can feel it. Makes my baby hairs stand up sometimes."

I sighed. He was just high, dopey Jed. He hadn't arranged for anyone to pretend to get shot. He couldn't even arrange to bring himself to the doctor. "Thanks, Jed. Bye!" I waved at him and trotted back to my car. One mystery solved. I loved tying up loose ends, although I still didn't have the jewels or know where Peyton was, and I had a nagging hunch the two were connected somehow.

I splayed my fingers outside my window as I drove, riding the air like waves. My radio was cranked and crackled out a passable version of 4 Non Blondes' "What's Up." I chanted along in my tinny, off-key singing voice and felt empowered and capable. I loved it when meteorological forces converged to send me a decent radio signal. First, I stopped at Gina's and tended to the animals. Leif had already walked Luna when he got off work, but I took her out again and made her promise to play nice with Tiger Pop.

193

After I showered cat and dog with attention, I hopped back into my brown Toyota and cruised the three miles home. I pulled into my driveway and quickly checked my house for more vandalism or excrement. I had about four hours of daylight left, and I had a lot to do. My house seemed untouched, so I quickly watered my plants and checked my caller ID. No one had called, not even a telemarketer. I felt a little bit sorry for myself, and for a second I was grateful that I had all this excitement in my life. It was better than being lonely. I quickly dismissed that thought, though. I wasn't lonely, I was alone, and there was nothing wrong with that.

Not that it hadn't occurred to me more than once that a government-sponsored dating program wouldn't be a welcome addition to the tax rolls. I was a cynic about men, but I never stopped hoping that there were some good ones out there. I just didn't have the time or patience to sift through the chaff looking for them.

I had a theory that if Big Brother got involved, the whole process could be streamlined. When a person turned eighteen, s/he would sign up for the Selective Service. (The military would have to get a new name for their deal, since "Selective Service" is too perfect for a dating organization.) Entrants would have to enter and keep current basic information—education level, one joke they think is funny, profession, where they stand on performing oral sex, whether or not they like or want kids, why their last relationship ended, et cetera. They would also have to come up with at least three previous relationship testimonials, unless they had never dated or had dated fewer than three people.

Not only would this hold us more accountable in how we acted in current relationships—because we would know the person we were with could be writing a dating reference for us tomorrow—it would also provide a database of people who are single and looking not to be, thus broadening our search area. After all, what are the odds of your soul mate living within sixty miles of where you are now, and of accidentally running into him or her in some leg of your daily routine? I wondered how one would go about getting legislation like that passed. I'd have to add it to my to-do list.

Meanwhile, I had some lawn to mow. I had always liked cutting the lawn. The hum and snort of the engine was soothing, and the results were organizationally breathtaking, particularly on this property with the rolling hills and sprawling trees. It would give me some downtime to riffle through my thoughts on the jewels and Peyton.

I switched to jogging shorts and a tank top and trotted down to the leaning red shed where I housed the mower. I gassed up the old Snapper rider, checked the oil, and cleaned out the area around the blade. I also loop-knotted my purse to the square handlebars so I could grab the tape of Nikolai and listen to it once I found my rhythm. I revved up the mower and started juicing grass, missing the familiar form of Luna jogging alongside. I couldn't wait to get me and my animals back here.

I jostled and purred around the lawn in front of the house for about an hour, being careful to reverse direction when I rode close to my gardens so I wouldn't shoot weed seeds into them. While steering, I held the tape recorder up to my ear and listened to the interview again. Nothing caught my attention except the confirmation of what I already knew—that Jed was the body planter and neither he nor Nikolai knew what had happened to Peyton. I re-gassed after about an hour and a half of mowing and moved to the area between the barn and sheds.

When I finished, the mosquitoes and gnats were starting to circle like sharks and the sun was setting, drawing shades of lavender across the horizon. I puttered the mower back into the shed and stretched, my legs shaky from three hours on a vibrating vehicle. I started to untie my purse when it occurred to me that I hadn't mowed the little patch of lawn down along the shoreline that led to Shangri-La. I hated backtracking, but it would be a nice feeling of completion to have it all freshly mown.

I left my purse untied on my lap and cruised down the driveway, bumping along the gravel. The trees formed a natural archway, and the fairy light of dusk shimmered through the leaves and made the path surreal. I could smell pollen in the air, and I was happy to be outdoors, tending to the earth.

When I reached my destination, I killed the motor so I could pick up some Diet Coke cans and candy wrappers that had been tossed onto the patch of grass. I glanced back into the deepening woods, away from Shangri-La, to where I had been carried during the magic show on the island. I was curious to see whether the bongo that had been my transport was still there, so I switched off the mower and tracked through the trees and brush, prickly ash and raspberry branches grabbing at my skin like hungry children.

I realized I was still holding my purse and the pop cans, so I shoved the cans down in the hobo bag, crinkling a stack of construction paper. It was the pictures Peyton had given me—one of the house, one of the animal, and one of the math lab. Tears burned in my eyes as I was reminded of her, and something scratched at the back of my head. I was overlooking a clue, I knew it, but I couldn't quite get at it. It was a dancing finger pointing at an ever-moving fog, and I could only catch brief glimpses of the image it was trying to show me.

I shook my head, stashed the drawings back in the purse, and slid the strap over my shoulder so my hands were free to push aside branches. When I reached the spot where first I and then the ringmaster had been deposited, there was no sign that we had ever been there. I only knew it was the right spot because it was at the base of the intertwined elms, the ones that looked like two people making out. Then I realized it: I was looking at the kissing tree that Regina had referred to in her code!

I dug around in my purse and pulled out Ron's translation, my hands shaking with excitement:

With your back to the kissing tree walk seven steps northwest kneel 23 left 12 right 11 left.

I backed against the kissing tree and shimmied around until I was facing halfway between the campground on the north side of the lake and the setting sun. I walked seven long steps and knelt. On my right was an oak tree and on my left was a rise covered in rotting leaves and poison ivy. Shit. For all I knew, there was nothing but dirt under there, or maybe a rusting piece of farm machinery, a common sight in Minnesota woods. Were the potential jewels enough reason to dig in a nest of poison ivy?

My best bet would be to go back to the house and fetch a long-sleeved shirt and some gardening gloves so the ivy wouldn't smack me, but I didn't have the patience for that, and it would be dark soon. I scoured around for a nice long stick and went back to poke at the pile. I heard the scrape of wood on metal. At least I knew that the pile was more than just dirt. I hooked an arm of the branch on the base of a poison ivy plant and pulled, hoping to remove enough so that I could get at what was underneath. I managed to pull up the ivy, along with about twenty feet of root spreading in each direction. The bastard was here to stay.

I dropped the branch and calculated how long it would take to reach the lake to rinse the poison off me if I just dug in real quick and peeked at what was buried there. I had the trip clocked at about three minutes if I used sand to scour the poison oil off my skin once I reached the water. I knelt down and stretched out my hand into the glistening leaves of three. That's when I heard voices coming down the road from Shangri-La. It was Sam and Jason, and they were headed straight for me.

EIGHTEEN

I HAD THREE OPTIONS: run, hide, or stroll out and act like hanging out in the woods was no big deal. I didn't think I could outrun Jason, and I figured I could always try the strolling thing if hiding didn't work, so I darted away from the kissing tree and toward the lake, crouching down and hugging my back to the wide base of an oak. My heart was hammering like a hummingbird's, and my fear level rose as I heard Jason's voice coming close enough to make out what he was saying.

"What sort of dumb bitch leaves a lawn mower out? She could at least finish the job."

"Maybe she just stopped to take a leak."

"Maybe I'll put a leak in her head if I come across her."

I bit my lip and felt my eyes get hot. That's when I remembered I had my purse, which meant I had my stun gun. I reached in, careful not to disturb the cans and paper and draw attention to myself. I felt the hard plastic and slowly drew out my weapon. I looked down gratefully and was shocked to see I had grabbed the tape recorder. I almost tossed it back in, but instead set it on the ground, timing my movement with Jason and Sam's footstep so I could hit the record button on a downfall.

If they were going to maul me, at least it would be on tape for some savvy police officer to find. Maybe, in an absurd punch line to my life, Ody and Gary Wohnt could stumble across it in some flurry of teamwork and talk about what a lousy date I was while they listened to it.

I set the recorder down, turned the volume knob as high as it would go, covered the non-microphone part of the small unit with some rotting leaves, and dug my hand back in my purse. This time I found the prize: the Z-Force, which had worked so well on Jed and his accomplice when they first carried me back here. I cradled it in my hand and concentrated on making myself disappear.

"So who told you that's what the code said?" Jason's voice sounded about twenty feet away. Judging by the intensity of his tone, he was excited.

"Some old couple staying on the island. I saw them doing a cross-word puzzle and asked them if they'd solve a puzzle I had. They knew right away what it was." I sensed pride in her voice, but it was lost on Jason.

"A bunch of bullshit nonsense is what it is. What sort of dumb-ass leaves a heap of jewelry in the woods for eighty years and then leaves some secret message to find it?"

Sam's tone was defensive. "She wasn't a total dumbass. She was just a little wacko. What's a rich lady supposed to do with a bunch of stolen jewelry, anyhow? She couldn't wear it, and she couldn't sell it with it being so hot. She just never got around to coming back for it. Leaves more for us."

They were about fifteen feet away now, and they had stopped walking. I guessed they were near the kissing tree. I prayed that Jason knew which way was northwest and didn't accidentally lurch across me. Outside of the woods, the sun was still halfway above the horizon, but in here, there was more shadow than light. I tried to calm myself with the hope that the darker it got, the harder I would be to see, but the more I focused on breathing, the harder it was to breathe at all.

"Okay, walk seven steps northwest. I'm sure it's seven girl steps."

"Which way is northwest?"

I could almost hear him point, the tension dripping in the air. He was trying to be stern, but he was desperately excited.

"You see anything?"

"Gawd, Jason, you're right behind me. *You* see anything? Huh?" She sounded angry, and her gum snapped in the air. "Like that big pile under the weeds? Duh?"

There was the smack of hard skin on soft, and I heard Sam squeak. He must have slapped her. "Hold this," he growled. I heard the thump of someone heavy dropping to the ground and then the sound of roots being pulled and dirt being moved. He apparently didn't notice that the plants he was ripping up were poison ivy.

"Do you see anything?" Sam's voice was overly eager as she tried to compensate for upsetting him.

"It's a goddamn safe the size of Fort Knox." He laughed, more startled than happy. "How did the old bag get this out here?"

"She said the Addamses ordered it when all the jewelry was disappearing but decided to sell the whole damn place instead. Her husband and some workers she paid to keep quiet moved it and buried all but the front of it, but she never told me where."

"Crazy bitch."

"Yeah, crazy bitch." Sam laughed childishly.

"It's a good thing you got that job nursing her, honey. That was a good thing. Can you shine that light over here? I got the lock uncovered."

Suddenly the forest was lit up. They must have brought a torch light. I felt big and obvious and ground my shoulder blades into the tree. I even considered closing my eyes on the time-honored principle that if you can't see them, they can't see you.

"What's the code, baby?"

I heard the crinkle of paper. "Twenty-three left, twelve right, eleven left. Is it turning okay?"

"Not hardly. Hand me the weasel piss." A squirting sound like juicy hair spray was followed by the whirring noise of a lock turning. "There she is!"

"Lemme see!"

"Back off! Give me that light!"

There was the groan of a door opening, yet fighting to retain inertia. Then, Sam's scream pierced the fading light of night, and the disorienting flash of brightness followed by dark told me she had dropped the light.

"There's a person in there!"

Cripes, I thought. How many fake dead bodies could one small area house in a week? Odds were, if there was really a person in there, she could pull the mask off it like it was a Scooby Doo villain to find out who the real crook was.

"A dead body can't hurt you. Goddammit!" The brightness from the flashlight steadied, and I heard the sound of something dry scraping against metal, followed by a grunt of a laugh. "Geez, I can't believe he still smells. There's even some body juice in here yet. Must be the old bag's husband."

Sam retched. "Gawd, that reeks. How come he's not just bones?"

"I dunno, but that Mrs. Krupps was a piece of work. She has him help drag the safe out to hide her stolen jewels in, and then she buries him in it. Real nice. The crazy old coot deserved what she got."

"She didn't deserve to die. She was an old lady, not hurting no one. She wasn't going to live much longer anyhow."

"I made sure of that, didn't I? And 'harmless old lady' my ass. She was a crook and a murderer, no better'n me. I think the two of us would have gotten along just fine."

"If you hadn't killed her."

"Shut your pie hole. Why can't you let anything drop? What the . . . here it is!"

"What?"

"Whoo-eee! Look at this pile! Would you look at it? Jesus. There must be a million dollars worth of jewels in here. It's like a god-damn pirate's treasure."

I couldn't stand it any longer. I peered one eye around the corner of my hiding tree, hopeful that Jason would be too distracted by the jewels to notice any movement in the darkening woods. I was right. He was kneeling over a rotting cloth bag, all but drooling as he stared inside. Sam was leaning over his shoulder and shining the light in the bag, causing green, red, and white reflections to dance off both their faces. Off to the side was a dark crumple of shape. The body technically could be anyone, but given that Mrs. Krupps's husband had disappeared about the same time she left the area, it was a safe bet that Jason was right and the corpse was indeed Mr. Krupps. The sweet, poisonous smell of rotted flesh wafted over to me.

"Can I touch 'em, Jason?"

"You can wear 'em, baby!" He spanked a tiara on her head, and she performed the beauty queen walk that every girl over the age of four can execute in her sleep. Jason nodded approvingly and fondled the gems in the bag. "These are just the beginning, baby. We invest these in the shit we need to get the meth lab going, and we'll never have to work another day in our lives. Hot damn, we can probably hire people to run the lab for us!"

The fog the finger in my head had been pointing at cleared. I saw Peyton standing behind Jason as he talked on his cell phone at the turtle races. Next to that was an image of her drawing of the math lab, only it wasn't a math lab, it was a meth lab. Of course that term would have no meaning for a little girl, so she had reworked it into something familiar. Jason must have found out she knew about the lab and snatched her. Now that I had a lead on Peyton, my armor fell away and I realized I didn't care about the jewels at all if I could find her. In fact, I'd trade all the money in the world to save her, but first, I needed to get out of here so I could tell the police what I knew.

That's when a finch flew right into the oak tree two over from where I was hiding. Those damn little birds must be the Jerry Lewises of the avian world, or else I emit some disorienting signal that only birds can hear. I pulled my head back and clamped down on my breath.

The bird's impact made a tiny noise, more like the pop of a knuckle cracking than the bang of a collision, but it was enough to burn the smile from Jason's voice and get him to his feet. "If any-goddamn-body is hiding over there, they best speak up and save themselves some bones!"

I slowly levered myself up using only my feet and the tree and prepared to run. If Jason walked in my direction, I would scream at the top of my lungs and take off like a banshee. I carefully dropped my purse off my shoulder and gently rested it on the ground to increase my aerodynamics. The zapper I kept in my right hand.

Jason tromped over toward me, and I could hear him scratching himself. The poison oil was beginning its assault on his skin. "Fe, fi, fo, fum, I smell the blood of somebody whose ass I'm gonna kick!"

I had an inappropriate, crazy urge to pee or sing. As he came closer on my left, I wiggled around the right side of the tree, staying just out of his peripheral vision. I was a quarter of the way around when Sam shrieked. "There's someone behind that tree!"

I charged out from my not-so-hiding spot and beat cheeks for the road. If I could get near Shangri-La, I could attract enough attention to stop Jason. If I didn't escape these woods, Peyton was as good as dead. There were about forty feet of forest before the clearing, and I devoured them like a fat man at a Chinese buffet.

Unfortunately, Jason was hungrier than me and grabbed me by the hair, snapping my head back, before I covered even twenty feet. I was hopelessly deep in the woods and it was too dark to see more than dim shapes.

Jason whipped me around until we were face to face and slapped me open-handed. The force was so strong it made everything a blank, and I was surprised to find myself crumpled on the forest floor, my stun gun lost. He kicked me in the stomach, and my diaphragm locked up, unable to pull in air for my lungs. I thought I heard Sam screaming, but it could have been me.

"That good enough for you, Mira?" He towered over me, his voice jarringly calm. "You think I'm insane? You think I'm a crazy man? Everyone has some insanity in them. Some of 'em hide it good, like old lady Krupps, and some of 'em don't, but we all got it. And now it's your turn to get it."

He kicked some dirt in my face, blinding me, and I pulled myself away from the sound of his voice. I bumped up against a tree and tried to drag my body erect. I felt nauseated and my mouth was salty with blood, but there was surprisingly little pain. I sucked at little bits of air as my diaphragm spasmed.

"Where you going in such a hurry? We've saved a little room here for you. Sam, open the front of the safe."

I heard the creak of the safe door and threw up, not able to swallow it back before it leaked out the corners of my mouth. I was beyond terrified. He was going to bury me alive in the safe, and no one was going to stop him. I hobbled a little away from the tree in my hunched-over position and pulled myself up. Jason slapped me again, returning me to the forest floor.

"Fucker," I grunted.

"What's that, Mira? You got something to say to me?"

A picture of Peyton formed in my mind, smiling up at me as I read her *Prince Cinders*. We were both safe in the children's section of the library, far from this madman. I concentrated on this image to remain conscious and reached deep into my reserves. My hand scrabbled around on the ground until I connected with a rock about the size of a grapefruit. My eyes had cleared enough to tell me that it was a white rock, and I hoped it wasn't too obvious in the dark. I dug at it, peeling my forefinger and thumbnails back in my desperation to hold it. "You're a fucker."

"I can't quite hear you. You must have some last words before you go to sleep forever, eh, baby?" His voice was lilting, soft and comforting.

He kneeled beside me, and I turned my heavy head toward his voice. "Yeah, I want to say that you're a sad, lonely bastard, and no one will ever respect you." At least that's what I said in my head. The reality of it was I focused all my fading consciousness on the rock in my hand. It came free and I slammed it into his face. He tumbled back in surprise. I took advantage, levering myself off the ground with a burst of adrenaline. Using both hands, I brought the rock down on his head, all the anger and loneliness that I had gathered in my lifetime joining with my fears for a little girl who was terrified and was me.

An ultrahuman strength powered my arms, and if I had connected directly with Jason's head, I would have split him in two like the waters of the Red Sea parted for Moses. As it was, he turned at the last millisecond, and the rock glanced the corner of his forehead with enough force to peel off a chunk of skin and knock him out. If the rock made a noise when it connected, I didn't hear it, but I did see Jason's eyes widen in surprise and then fog over as he passed out, face down in the dirt.

I watched for a moment as the leaves closest to his mouth fluttered with his breath, and I convinced myself I could actually see the side of his head start to swell. The goose egg looked promising, like maybe it would grow to the size of an elephant's testicle. I staggered back and looked wildly around for more attackers. Sam was leaning against the kissing tree. She pulled an Eve Slim out of the pocket of her polo shirt and lit it.

"Wanna split the jewels?"

I couldn't recall what she was talking about, but I was sure I wasn't in a sharing mood. "No."

She sighed. "Didn't think so."

She brushed off her behind and strolled back the way she came. I scrabbled in the near dark for the tape recorder and then limped after her, my foot kicking on something on the forest floor. It was the stun gun, barely visible through my dirt-flecked eyes. I leaned over to grab it, the exertion shooting needles of pain through my bruised torso, and limped back to Jason. I zapped him once, just to make sure my Z-Force hadn't been broken in the scuffle. His body spasmed and he groaned, but his breathing stayed constant. It was a crying shame.

NINETEEN

I HOBBLED OUT OF the woods and toward Shangri-La. Jason wasn't a clever man. He had come to town for jewels, found a secret room, and decided it would be a perfect spot for a meth lab, probably for all the same reasons the original architect thought it would make an ideal rum room. Once he found the jewels, millions of dollars worth of jewels, he still intended to start a meth lab in that room. This lack of creativity told me he was also likely using the hidden room to hide Peyton.

Every step I took attacked my head like a piranha, and I wouldn't have made it if a couple out walking hadn't seen me stumble out of the woods. The woman stayed with me while the man ran to Shangri-La to call the police. He promised me he would look for Peyton in the master bedroom closet the minute he got off the phone.

The police beat the ambulance. When I explained what had happened, particularly about the dead body back there ("No, I know. But this one really *is* dead.") and my hunch about Peyton's whereabouts, the state police were called in. Unfortunately, the press was never far behind them, so several grotesque pictures of me were snapped before the paramedics whisked me off to the hospital. I made some crack that they better not lose me like they did the dwarf, but they didn't think it was funny.

Luckily, the photos of me never made it into any paper. I was pushed aside for photographs of the happy reunion between Peyton and Leylanda. The man who had called the police went to the master bedroom as he had promised, and he found Peyton tied to a chair in the hidden room, her mouth gagged. He also found a TV on in front of her and a pile of candy and potato-chip wrappers underfoot. Apparently Sam had spoiled her rotten, turning on cartoons and feeding her whatever she wanted as long as she agreed not to yell. Peyton was quoted as saying, "It was the best time I ever had."

At the hospital, my x-rays showed a mild concussion and severe bruising, but no broken bones. Eating mostly carbohydrates really did pay off. Jason was still unconscious when he was loaded into the second ambulance and driven to the hospital. Like me, he had a mild concussion, though he needed four stitches in his head. That made me the winner. As a sweet bonus, Jason also had the worst case of poison ivy on record in the five-state area. He required prednisone shots to keep his throat from closing up and had to have his hands strapped down to keep from scratching. They actually took photographs of his oozing sores to use in some medical textbook.

When I handed my tape recording of Jason confessing to killing Regina over to the police, he was pretty much assured of some jail time for murder, but Samantha Beladucci, aka Sam Krupps, cemented that reality. When the state police caught her about to cross into Wisconsin, she cooperated fully. She would serve some time for aiding and abetting, but Jason was going to go away for a long, long time.

Sam's story proved it had gone down just like I thought. Regina had stolen the jewels and then hidden them in the safe in the woods. Autopsy results showed her husband had taken a severe blow to the head, but actual cause of death was inconclusive due to the age of the remains. It was safe to assume that Regina had killed him. If she was crazy enough to do that, she was certainly crazy enough to leave a wealth of jewels hidden in the woods in rural Minnesota. This made me wonder what the stash of rhinestones I had hidden at my childhood home said about my mental health, but I saw no reason to dwell on that. Sam heard the story of the hidden jewels when she was caring for Regina and told Jason.

For Sam and Jason, the *Star Tribune* contest to find the planted necklace was an unhappy coincidence. Jason found out about it when he called to set aside the master bedroom at Shangri-La. Kellie Gibson had assumed he was reserving it to get a head start on the contest and had asked him as much. He played along like that was really why he was coming, but he was fuming at the attention and number of people it brought, particularly since, according to Sam, he had just gotten out of jail in Texas for possession of methamphetamines and wasn't supposed to leave the state.

Kellie had inadvertently provided a distraction for Jason's nefarious activities, since she had booked the Romanov troupe. Her third cousin's husband, Jim Neville, aka Nikolai Romanov, ran a traveling circus in the South, and Kellie was talked into hiring them to come to Battle Lake, and specifically to Shangri-La, to put on a show people would never forget. When a scheming Jason approached Mr.

Neville and played on his supersized ego, it was only too easy to convince the little guy to stage his own death. He was an actor, after all.

Meanwhile, Jason tore apart the master bedroom closet and found the secret room right away, but he couldn't find anything that would lead him to the jewels. He decided to make lemonade out of his lemons and began to gather what he needed to start a meth lab. He knew the resort was empty in the off-season, as the Gibsons flew down to Arizona every winter. The rum room would be perfect for manufacturing meth, which Jason figured would make him rich and supply plenty of the dangerous drug to feed his own addiction. Unfortunately, at the turtle races Peyton overheard him on the phone talking to a friend about what he'd need to start his own operation, and she kept asking him what a "math lab" was.

Once Jason realized he could lose the jewels *and* the dream of his own meth lab if Peyton narced him out, he decided to silence her. Sam was queasy about harming a child, though, and convinced Jason to wait until the box in Whiskey Lake was found. Then, she argued, there would be a lot fewer people and photographers around, and it would be a lot easier to dispose of a body. Jason agreed.

When Sam got a couple at Shangri-La to break the secret code that Jason had stolen from my purse, he knew exactly what "the kissing tree" was referring to, since he had spent a lot of time hunting in Sunny's woods and even had a stand in the tree for a while.

And the rest of it I caught on tape. Sam vehemently denied that they'd planted the fake body in the lake or shot the little man. That was one mystery the police would never solve, and I saw no payoff in revealing the truth of those riddles to the law. I reminded myself to have Jed remove the second fake body, the one he had planted last night, before someone stumbled across it.

When I got released from the hospital that same night, I reclaimed Luna and Tiger Pop from Gina's and went straight home to sleep in my own bed for the first time in days. It was glorious. I was naked and comfortable, and Tiger Pop purred away between my feet. I was supposed to be diving for the box and splitting the reward with Nikolai that very night, but it wasn't going to happen. I don't know if he showed up at our designated spot, because I never heard from him again. Probably there is a theatrical dwarf somewhere cursing my name right now.

I stopped by the library the next morning to ask Mrs. Berns if she'd mind if I took the day off. She happily agreed to hold down the fort whenever I needed it. Unfortunately, she was wearing a see-through blouse with no bra when she told me this. Her large nipples peeked at me like myopic stomach eyes. I tracked down Kennie and hired her to tell Mrs. Berns that she must wear undergarments with her transparent clothing. As an afterthought, I also asked her to "pull a Jason" on Leif, Gina's husband. Kennie was to get him fall-down drunk and then take pictures of him and her in compromising positions. I encouraged her to enlist Mrs. Berns's help in this endeavor.

"Don't actually do anything with him, Kennie. I just need the pictures for blackmail, something to keep him honest."

"Sure, sugar pie. I won't actually do anything with him." She winked as she said this, and I wondered if it was evil that I was setting Leif up for the most humiliating night of his life, one that he would only be able to remember snatches of. An image of Gina's tear-swollen face flashed through my head, and I decided that I was just helping out the great karma machine in the sky. Once Leif sobered up, I would show him the photos of him getting jiggy with

Kennie and Mrs. Berns and threaten to publish them in the *Recall* if I ever heard of him cheating on Gina again.

Kennie promised to do the deeds as soon as she got done leading her As Good As Gold on the Otter Tail River Tour. Apparently, the Minnesota Nice business wasn't doing as well as expected. People felt too guilty about hiring someone else to do their dirty work and decided to go back to the tried-and-true practices of avoidance and denial. To supplement her income, Kennie had started a gold-panning business on the Otter Tail River. There was no gold in the river, and Kennie got around that fact by trademarking the term "As Good As Gold" to refer to any of various types of river rocks. I promised to hand her brochures out at the library and go out on one more outing with her and Gary as payment for the favors she was doing for me. Apparently, I had gone over like gangbusters with Ody, and he wanted to take me fishing before he returned to Alaska. How much worse could my reputation in town get? At least I knew our time together had an expiration date.

I knew I needed more time to heal before I went diving, but by the next afternoon, the need to satisfy my curiosity outweighed the need to be pain-free. I borrowed Jed's diving equipment and got permission from the landowners to take off from the creek on the north side of the lake. My bruises made swimming slow going, but eventually I found the camo netting about seventy-five feet straight out and twenty-one feet straight down, just like Nikolai predicted. If not for him, I would have passed right over it, since the greenish-gray cover blended perfectly with the lake bottom if you weren't looking for it.

The box underneath the camo cover was light once I loosed it from the rope and anchor mooring it. I started swimming back before I decided I should bring the rope and netting back with me, too. No reason to litter the lake. I wasn't able to open the box on my own, so I called the *Star Tribune*. They were grateful someone had finally found it, and the timing was perfect, what with all the publicity Peyton's abduction and subsequent return and Regina Krupps's stolen jewelry were getting. They ran a front-page story on the "Real Jewels of the North Country," and the featured photo was of Peyton draped in the jewels.

I felt momentarily bad that Nikolai wasn't getting any of the money for finding the box, and then I realized I had promised him only that I would not keep more than half. By the end of the week, a "secret donor" had arranged for all the cabins at the Last Resort to be painted, inside and out. I also arranged for a deluxe Scrabble game, complete with a lazy Susan, to be sent to the Fortune Café.

The children's section at the library got completely revamped as well—new chairs, new stuffed animals, new equipment for watching movies and listening to books on tape, and a cavalcade of happy, colorful new books. Peyton received a colossal box of Sugar Lips Wax Chewing Gum, Strawberry Pop Rocks, Razzles Candy Gum, and chocolate cigarettes in the mail. When I spoke to her the day after she was found, she told me the kidnapping was really fun. She said the only downside was the crabby man who had to tie her up even though she would have stayed anyways. I had no reason to doubt this, and apparently Leylanda heard this too and took it to heart, because she loosened up a little on her daughter and let her keep the candy. She even let Peyton chew gum in the library.

Those donations took up a big chunk of the contest money, and I figured not spending all the money on myself was the same as not keeping it. With what was left, I paid my bills three months out, leaving just enough to hire a landscaper to do some touch-up work at my place. I called Swenson's Nursery, and Johnny promised he would be over before the end of the week. I felt conspicuous enough requesting him specifically and after hours, so I refrained from offering extra for shirtlessness.

While I waited for him to show up on a beautiful Friday evening, I phoned my mom. When Peyton had been kidnapped, some more of my heart froze. What I hadn't known was how much it was going to thaw when she was found. My mom and I hadn't talked in over a year, but there's something about worrying about kids and getting the shit beat out of you that makes you want to hear your mom's voice.

"Mira?"

"Yeah. Sorry I haven't called in a while, Mom."

"How're you doing?" She sounded so grateful that it brought tears to my eyes.

"I've been pretty good. How about you?"

I heard her weigh her options, and she chose to keep it light, even though she couldn't keep the emotion out of her voice. I suppose she didn't want to scare me off again. "I'm real good. We're having a wedding shower for your cousin next weekend. We'd love to see you."

"Yeah, maybe. I'd like to see you, too." The funny thing was, I meant it. My mom and I had drifted apart after my dad died, no doubt about it. Or maybe I had pushed her away. But now she seemed too far away. I was relieved it wasn't too late to change that.

"You still have Tiger Pop?"

"Yeah, she's on my lap right now." I stroked her soft fur. "I'll give you a call about next weekend, 'kay?"

"That'd be nice. I love you, Mira."

The tears were rolling down my face now. This had been a damn tough week, but my mom still loved me. I made my voice sound strong. "I love you too, Mom." I clicked the phone off and dug my face into Tiger Pop's clean fur.

When Johnny showed up a half hour later, I was composed and wearing my sexiest fellow-gardener-cum-natural-woman look—no makeup save for lip gloss, hair loose around my shoulders, a white tank top, and faded cutoffs. The lightness of my clothes accented the fading, greenish-yellow bruises on my face and arms. I was still stiff from the beating but feeling whole and strong. I hardly made a fool of myself the whole time Johnny was over.

He spent more time admiring my gardens and giving me tips on improved water retention and maximization of sunlight than actually landscaping, but it was a wonderful evening. Once, I caught him staring at the rainbow of marks spattered across my face and neck. I had to glance away, the angry and protective look in his eyes too much for my emotional state.

I instead got Johnny to talk about himself some. Turns out he wasn't kicked out of college, either for knifing someone or for stealing plants, though he did write his senior paper on the blade tree, a plant native to Bolivia. When he graduated with his BS in plant biology, he wanted to go on to grad school to get his PhD. He'd seen himself as either a professor or an activist, but before he decided what college he wanted to do his doctoral work at, his dad was diagnosed with terminal stomach cancer. Johnny returned to Battle Lake to help his mom take care of his dad and was making the best of his current life working at the nursery, giving piano lessons, and playing with a local band.

"Mira?"

I was walking Johnny to his car. The sun was setting the lake on fire as it dropped in, clouds of pink and orange rising like steam on the horizon.

"Yeah?"

"Can I ask you something personal?"

My heart skipped and dropped. I clenched my teeth to hold back the slew of dumb babbling suddenly pushing to escape my mouth. "Sure."

"Are you dating Ody?"

I think I might have laughed, but it came out like a horse bark. "No. I was just doing Kennie a favor."

Johnny looked relieved, then amused. He reached out as if to touch my face, shook his head once quickly, and stuffed his hands in his worn jean pockets. "I'm sorry someone did this to you, Mira."

My heart tumbled. "Thanks. But I'll heal. I always do."

"It was a good night, tonight. I had fun with you."

I smiled. "I had fun with you, too."

Johnny didn't give me a bill at the end of our wonderful evening, but immediately after he left, I wrote out a check and dropped it in the mailbox at the end of my mile of driveway, retrieving the day's mail at the same time. I wanted an excuse to walk down the road barefoot. On my way back, I slowed to scratch my feet in the soft sand pool, an unexplained spot in every country driveway where the sand is so smooth it almost feels wet. I decided when I got back to the house, I'd eat some fresh peas, drink a Dr. Pepper, and watch *Thelma and Louise*, one of three movies I owned. And maybe, if I had the time, I'd draw Johnny's name over and over again in a notebook and sketch hearts around it.

It was such a good night that I almost threw out the letter from the University of Minnesota I found among the bills before I even opened it. Instead, I studied the return address as I crunched down the gravel and smelled the dusty earth and listened to crickets sing. The letter was from the U of M's English department. I had blown off my studies since I had moved to Battle Lake in March, and I didn't see how this letter could be good news.

Curiosity, my only consistent vice, won over eventually, and when I reached my front deck I sat down and ripped open the letter, my toes digging into the still-warm earth of my front flower bed. The letter was from the one professor I had connected with at the university, Dr. Lindstrom. He was a literature professor who questioned everything and had a wonderfully dry sense of humor.

His letter was short and sweet:

Dear Mira:

You are missed! I hope you haven't gotten so involved in the active animal-rights movement up there in God's country that you can't give us a hand back here. I need a research assistant this fall, and you're my woman. Pay is meager, but your tuition would be free. Is it a deal? Respond at your convenience, as long as it is before August.

Sincerely yours,

Dr. Michael Lindstrom

I read the letter three times before I was convinced it wasn't a joke, and that's when I started to feel green around the gills. This would have been a no-brainer a month ago. An opportunity like this came once in a lifetime. Who wouldn't want to live in the Twin

Cities and go to school for free and eat at restaurants that didn't serve hot beef and white bread as their specials? But now, I wasn't so sure.

I stood up so abruptly that I scraped the back of my leg on the deck. I went into the house purposefully, crumpled up Dr. Lindstrom's letter, and tossed it in the garbage. I opened the fridge, fixed myself supper, and stuck *Thelma and Louise* into the VCR. I watched it until I was too tired to keep my eyes open, and then I popped off to bed, but not before I pulled Dr. Lindstrom's letter out of the garbage, smoothed it out, and set it on my kitchen table to look at again in the morning.

ACKNOWLEDGMENTS

I'm indebted to Ray and Diane for the alternating Mondays and Wednesdays they sacrifice so I can write without guilt, and for being adept copyeditors. Oh, and for telling me I could be whatever I wanted to be when I grew up. Also, there isn't a sufficiently big enough thank-you to give to Holly for being my first reader and best cheerleader, so I'm offering only a ten-point font thank-you and hoping she understands.

I am grateful to Joan Jung at the Hennepin County Medical Examiner's Office for gathering insight into the smell, juiciness, and overall condition of a body in the unusual state of decomposition it finds itself in within these pages, and for not turning me over to the FBI for asking.

Barbara, Brian, and Lisa, you are the dream team, turning out great books with brilliant covers and making sure that people read them—thank you. And thank you to Wade for always setting me straight on the eighties and toning down my myriad references to pooping and being on fire. You are a priceless resource. Jessica Morrell, your freelance editing is incisive, thorough, and encouraging.

Christine, I appreciate your neighborly ways, and Suzanna, many thanks for always feeding my sense of humor. Dr. Jen, I value your support in sales, signings, and kid-watching, as well as your deft adjustments. Finally, thank you to Zoë and Xander for wearing your costumes way past Halloween, for putting up with the "don't talk to Mom when she's reading or writing unless it's an emergency" rule, and for your fuzzy morning bedheads.

BOOK CLUB QUESTIONS

- In mystery writing, red herrings are potential suspects that throw you off the trail of the real killer. Who or what were the red herrings in *June Bug*, and which were the most successful in distracting the reader from the truth?

- In *June Bug* as well as in *May Day*, there are many strong female characters. Which are the most appealing, and why?

- What other strong female characters have you encountered in books? What are the similarities and differences between those characters and Mira James?

- Critics have described Mira James as having "a surfeit of sass," overflowing with "irreverent humor," and being "a little bit raunchy." What about her sense of humor appealed to you, and how did the generous use of comedy add to the book?

- The Murder-by-Month Mystery series is set in Battle Lake, Minnesota—a real town—and many of the landmarks, including the Chief Wenonga statue, actually exist. Does having the book take place in a real and intimate setting, one that you could visit or live in, add to or detract from its entertainment value? How so?

- What insights, mannerisms, or ways of speaking unique to Minnesota stood out for you? What other books set in the Midwest were you reminded of while reading *June Bug*?

- On what page did you solve the mystery? What clues did you use to dig out the truth?

- Have you ever eaten a Nut Goodie? If not, how long will it take you to get your hands on one?

Read on for an excerpt from the
next Murder-by-Month Mystery by Jess Lourey

Knee High by the 4th of July

COMING SOON FROM MIDNIGHT INK

IT WAS THE FIRST Thursday in July, the hottest month in Minnesota. The Channel 7 news, the only channel that came in clearly at my doublewide in the woods, was predicting the hottest July in history. The humid, sticky weather made the whole state feel like a greenhouse, or the inside of someone's mouth. As a direct result, people who had to work were cranky, people on vacation were ecstatic, and crops were growing like a house on fire. Locals said that if the corn were knee high by the Fourth of July, it would be a bumper crop. We were two days shy of that mark and the corn was already shoulder high on a grown man. That strangeness should have been a warning to us all.

There was a bright spot on the horizon, though. Every July, to celebrate the man who had named the town and the coming of his statue a couple hundred years later, Battle Lake hosted a three-day Chief Wenonga Days Festival. It was always scheduled the weekend closest to the Fourth of July so the town could double-dip on the tourists. Wenonga Days perennially included Crazy Days and a street dance on Friday; a kiddie carnival with turtle races, a parade, and fireworks on Saturday; and a bike race, pet-and-owner look-alike contest, 5K run, and all-town garage sale on Sunday. The planned revelry this year would be extraordinary, though, because the statue of the Chief had been in Battle Lake for exactly twenty-five years this July.

Ah, the Chief. Twenty-three well-sculpted feet of dark alpha male forever guarding the shores of Battle Lake. He was the perfect man if one overlooked the blatant racist stereotyping and the fact that he was a giant fiberglass statue. The Chief visited many a dream of mine, all strong and silent, sporting a full headdress, six-pack abs on a half-naked body, tomahawk in one hand, and the other hand raised in a perennial "How."

I pulled into my driveway after work and parked the car in the shade of the lilac bushes, near where both Tiger Pop, my calico kitty, and Luna, my German shepherd–mix foster dog, were resting. Luna thumped her tail and Tiger Pop opened one eye when I petted them, but that was about all the welcome home I got. I dropped my un-opened mail on the table inside the front door, changed Tiger Pop and Luna's water, dropped some ice cubes into their bowls, refilled their food, coaxed them into the stifling house, and apologized for neglecting them all day. They both plopped down on the cool linoleum near the refrigerator, and I considered joining them. The ant creeping across the floor nixed that idea. I tossed my jean shorts and tank top over the back of the couch and crawled naked onto my bed, a fan pointing at my head. The air it was moving around was so scorching that I would have been better off rigging up a flame-thrower.

I slept on top of the sheets, except for my feet, which I always covered in bed. Seeing *Roots* as a child had affected me to the point where I couldn't leave my feet vulnerable for fear of having them chopped off as I slept. I knew the sheets wouldn't stop an ax, but they made me feel safer, and after two months in Battle Lake, I needed all the reassurance I could get.

I woke up seven hours later with a layer of sweat covering me like a salty wool blanket. An icy shower and a quick breakfast of whole grain Total with organic raisins, and I was on my early way to meet another oppressively hot day. I knew my Wednesday "Mira's Musings" column in the *Battle Lake Recall* was going to be somehow related to the Wenonga Days planning meeting, so I needed to find out how it ended and get a draft of that out before I opened the library. Besides my regular filing, ordering, and organizing duties there, I wanted to take down the Fourth of July holiday decorations—the library would be closed on Saturday and Sunday—and replace them with generic summer ornamentation. Somewhere in there I also needed to find a recipe "representative of Battle Lake" (in Ron Sims's words) for that column. My to-do list for the day was getting as stifling as the hazy July air.

The fertile smell of the swamp I passed by on the gravel tickled my nose, and I could hear frogs singing in the sloughs. The sun was scratching the horizon when I turned right onto County Road 78, just up the street from the Shoreline Restaurant and Chief Wenonga. I had chosen this route because driving past the Chief on my way to town seemed like a natural way to get my (mental) juices flowing.

I was just onto the tar when a red tank zoomed over the hill and aggressively hugged my Toyota's bumper. Whoever it was had their brights on, unnecessary in the bright dawn and making it impossible for me to see their face in my rearview mirror. I was pretty sure it was a guy with a small penis, though. My feet twitched to tap my brakes, but it was too early in the morning to trade my safety for my pride. I pulled to the right to let the Humvee pass and glared at the silver-rimmed tires as they raced past me and my puddle jumper. Feeling cranky, I drove the last mile into town, cursing tourists and gas-guzzling army vehicles. I was moving on to getting mad at the color red when I crested the hill right before the Shoreline.

The restaurant's parking lot was peppered with a sprinkling of early-morning fishers in town for their excellent eggs Benedict and hash browns. My temper cooled a little as I thought of good food and the fact that I was just about to say a great good morning to my big fiberglass man. I leaned forward in my seat so I could spot him a millisecond sooner. Just beyond the brown roof of the Shoreline, I made out Chief Wenonga's cement stand, with four bolts poured into it. I didn't remember seeing the bolts before, and a beat later, I realized why. The bolts held Chief Wenonga up, one each in the front and back of his feet. Now that he was no longer there, the bolts were obvious.

Someone had stolen Chief Wenonga.

I screeched into the parking lot, threw myself out of the car, and ran to the Chief's stand. I touched the bolts, cool and wet with morning dew, and looked around frantically. Where were the police? Where was the ambulance? Why wasn't anyone doing anything? I could see the fishers eating their eggs through the picture windows of the Shoreline, their eyes happy, their mouths talking, as if someone important to us hadn't just been disappeared. Cars drove past on 78. Waves lapped at the shore of Battle Lake, and the sun was rising steadily through the morning mist. How could the world go on as if nothing were wrong? I was struck with an image of me slapping the Chief's photo on the back of milk cartons and attaching posters to interstate semis.

I swallowed a deep breath and squeezed my hands into fists. There must be a rational explanation for this. People don't kidnap ginormous fiberglass statues. Probably at the Wenonga Days planning meeting yesterday it had been decided that the Chief needed a cleaning, and workers had quickly driven him to some fiberglass statue detailing shop. Or maybe they had decided to add a "Find the Chief" contest to Wenonga Days. Or maybe . . . an icy finger traced a shiver down my spine.

My horror turned to anger, and then, thank God, to embarrassment. My Chief Wenonga obsession had clearly gotten out of hand. I made a mental note to find a new, more reliable fixation, and in the meanwhile, to visit the local coffee shop, the Fortune Café, to see what I could find out about the Chief's new location. I wiped my dew-covered hands on my shorts and marched back toward my car. When I reached for the door latch, a swath of red caught my eye. It was on my faded cut-offs, and it was the smear I had just left with my hand. Since when was dew red?

For a moment, I entertained the notion that the Chief had bled when he was removed from his posts. It made sense—in Crazy-land—as the posts were the only thing I had touched. It was the fiberglass stigmata. Then, good sense crept into my head, followed immediately by fear, and they both slid down my neck and back like cold oil. I had real blood on my hands.

ABOUT THE AUTHOR

Jess Lourey lives in Alexandria, Minnesota, where she teaches creative writing and sociology full time at the local college. When not raising her two wonderful kids, teaching, or writing, you can find her gardening, devouring novels, and navigating the niceties and meanities of small-town life. She is a member of Mystery Writers of America, Sisters in Crime, the Loft, and Lake Superior Writers.